Britain's Railways

in the seventies

North South East & West

PUBLISHED BY
IAN ALLAN LTD
TERMINAL HOUSE·SHEPPERTON·TW17 8AS·ENGLAND
TELEPHONE: WALTON-ON-THAMES 28484

Printed in the United Kingdom by Crampton & Sons Ltd, Sawston, Cambridge.

First published 1975

Cover: A Brush Class 47 2750hp Co-Co diesel-electric locomotive leaving Bath with a Bristol-Paddington train in the spring of 1970. *Ivo Peters*

Below: A combination of BRCW Class 26 and BR Class 25 Bo-Bos threading picturesque Killiecrankie Pass on the 11.30 Inverness-Glasgow train in June 1972. *J. H. Cooper-Smith*

THIS book is different from the main stream of Ian Allan railway picture books. It is different in several ways. First, and perhaps most importantly to the traditional railway enthusiast, its subject is not steam locomotives, although some steam pictures quite properly have their place in it. It is different also in that it is not confined to the trains or engines of a particular area, line, company, designer or BR region, nor even to British Rail itself. The only criterion for a picture's inclusion in this book, is that it must be a good picture of a railway in Britain going about its normal business.

Now for the reason for venturing away from the well-trodden and successful paths of railway pictorial publishing. No-one can deny that the newer forms of motive power lack the character and attraction of the steam locomotive and they are unlikely ever to inspire more than a fraction of the idolatry accorded to steam power, and steam railways in particular. Even so, although the numbers of devotees of early railways and steam locomotives continue to grow as more working engines and preserved lines are brought into use and leisure time is extended, they are being joined by an expanding band of a new breed of railway enthusiasts—for the railway of today and its promise of a less unpleasant environment in the future.

There is another quite important object of the book and that is to provide in effect a gallery in which those other rather specialised enthusiasts—the railway photographers—can display their arts. Oddly, although the various phenomena and techniques that would make the camera possible were known by the early 18th century, photography did not become fully practicable until over half way through the 19th, about 30 years after the first public railway started operation. But once railways and the camera became associated (a Locomotive Publishing Company photograph of GWR broad-gauge engines 0-6-0 *Alligator* and 2-2-2 *Argus* in about 1849 is said to be one of the earliest ever taken) railway photo-

Below: Class 26/1 No 5341 (26.041) at Kyle of Lochalsh with the 17.50 Kyle-Inverness train in June 1973. *G. R. Hounsell*

INVERGORDO

Above: At Invergordon in July 1972 a trainload of pipes en route for Tyneside to be coated with bitumastic before return to Scotland for use in a North Sea oil project. *British Rail*

graphy quickly developed as an individual art form and high reputations were established by many of its numerous exponents.

Understandably, the steam locomotive, with its variety and nostalgic associations, has received even in recent years greater attention from both photographers and publishers than the more utilitarian diesel and electric motive power units. But the photogenic qualities of the railway have never rested entirely on the steam locomotive and its withdrawal has not greatly diminished them. The train in its environment provides an infinitely more varied subject than the ship, the aeroplane or the road vehicle in theirs. So there is also a devoted band of railway photographers of modern traction, and their work greatly enriches the pages of railway periodicals. However, the periodicals have limited capacity and inevitably

many good pictures are born to blush unseen, except by the photographer and his intimates. This book serves the double purpose of rescuing well over a hundred excellent railway scenes from that fate and meeting the growing number of requests we, as the premier railway publishers, receive for more pictorial records of the railways of today at work.

During the early 1970s British Rail was carrying out a stock classification and renumbering programme; where given in the captions, the first numbers are those—some old, some new— the subjects bore when the pictures were taken and numbers in brackets are the old ones, or new ones issued subsequently. At the same time BR was getting well into a programme of withdrawal of certain locomotive classes and branch line and station closures. Consequently some of the subjects pictured in this book have by now disappeared or will soon be gone. We are gratified to have been able to provide the means of giving a wide public showing for the dedicated work of various photographers in capturing those scenes.

3

Above: Class 27 No 5389 (27.037) on the summer-only midday Mallaig-Fort William train in May 1972; it carries the Class 1 code despite having only two coaches. *J. H. Cooper-Smith*

Right: Another Class 27, No 5357 (27.011), almost in the clouds at Tyndrum Summit on a Crianlarich-Corpach timber train in May 1972. *J. H. Cooper-Smith*

Above: Restyled dmu at Arrochar & Tarbet on the 10.35 Glasgow-Oban train in June 1965. *G. A. Watt*

Below: Large snowplough powered by Class 26/1 No 5313 (26.013) at Aberdeen in November 1973. *C. J. M. Lofthus*

Right top: Class 26/1 No 5314 (26.014) with an Aberdeen-Inverurie goods train passing Dyce in October 1973. *C. J. M. Lofthus*

Right centre: Metro-Cammell dmu forming a Branch Line Society excursion as the last train to Ayr Goods Station in August 1971, passing one of the last rail-rail level crossings in the UK. *Derek Cross*

Right bottom: Two AM3 emus forming an 09.04 Cathcart Outer Circle departure from Glasgow Central in May 1975. *D. G. Cameron*

Left above: Class 27 No 27.017 (5353) leaving Oban Station with the 13.40 train to Glasgow in June 1975; the restyled dmu on the left will be the 18.55 departure for Glasgow. *G. A. Watt*

Left below: Class 27/1 Nos 5396 (27.108) and 5399 (27.110) with a Sunday 10.30 Glasgow-Edinburgh train in November 1973 leaving the main line at Winchburgh to avoid engineering work. *G. A. Watt*

Above: A truly rural setting in Princes Street Gardens, Edinburgh, as the 12.00 Glasgow-Edinburgh train passes, with Class 27/1 27.110 (5399) at the head and a second Class 27 at the rear. *G. A. Watt*

Above: Class 47/3 No 1881 (47.362) heading a Haverton Hill-Ardeer train of chemical tanks at Mauchline in July 1971. *Derek Cross*

Left: Another 47/3 No 1817 (47.336) at Polquhap Summit with a Linwood-Birmingham car conveyor in September 1971. *Derek Cross*

Right above: Class 26/1 No 5339 (26.039) on the 13.30 Aberdeen-Perth postal train in March 1974.
Brian Morrison

Right below: Class 37 No 6856 (37.156) passing Polmadie Depot, Glasgow, with a block oil train in September 1971 shortly before the section was electrified. *N. E. Preedy*

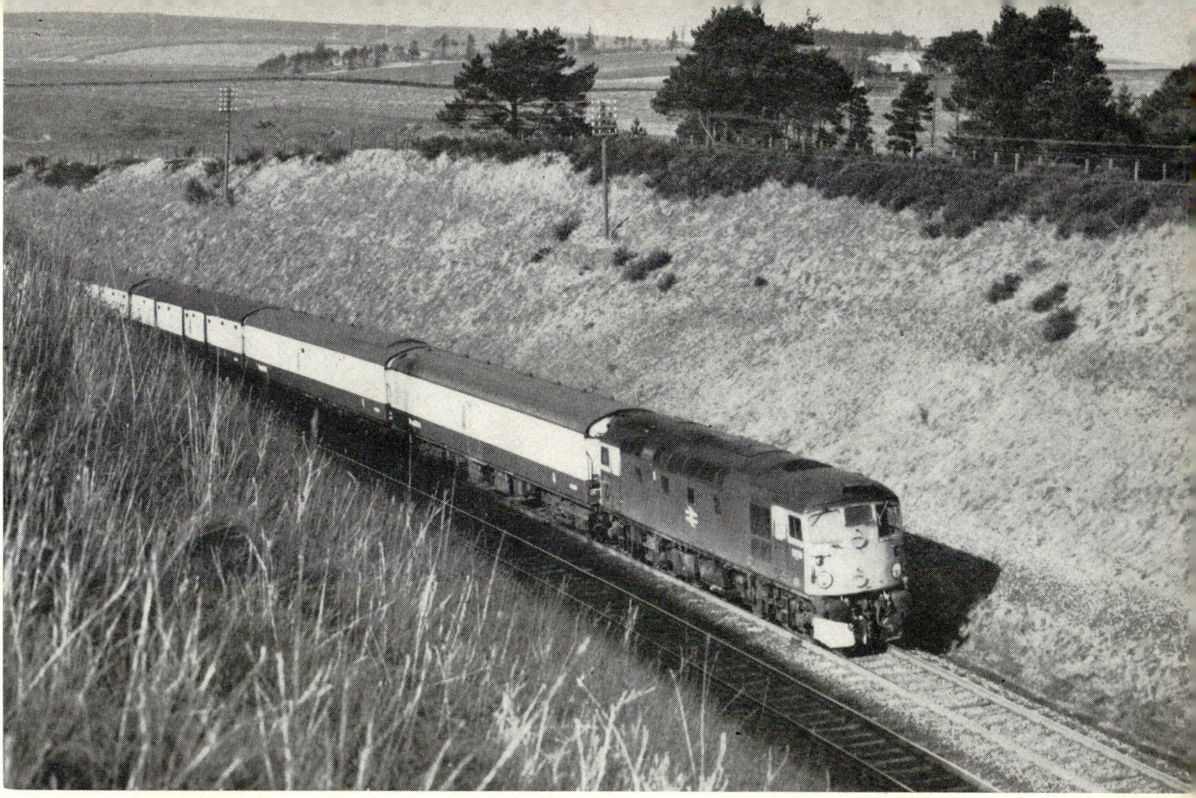

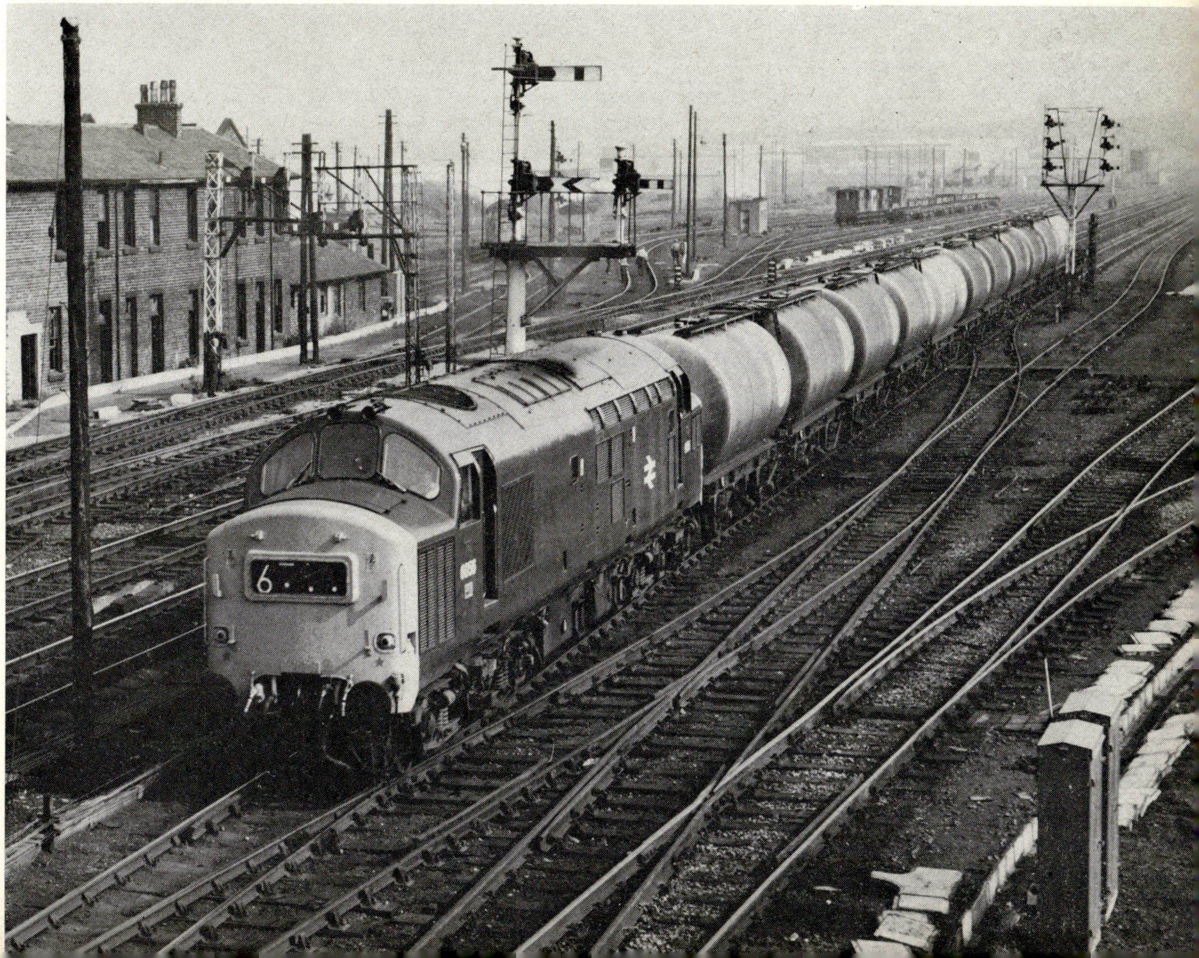
6

Above: A gaggle of diesel power at Polmadie Depot, Glasgow, in September 1971. *N. E. Preedy*

Left: Class 26 No 5305 (26.005) on a block coal train from Dalkeith Colliery in June 1972, with the partly dismantled Waverley Route to be seen at top left.
J. H. Cooper-Smith

Right above: English Electric Class 40 1Co-Co1 No 40.085 (285) at the head of the 13.10 Glasgow-Aberdeen train at Cadder in September 1974.
D. G. Cameron

Right: No 40.052 (252) passing Edinburgh Waverley with a down block cement train in June 1975.
C. J. M. Lofthus

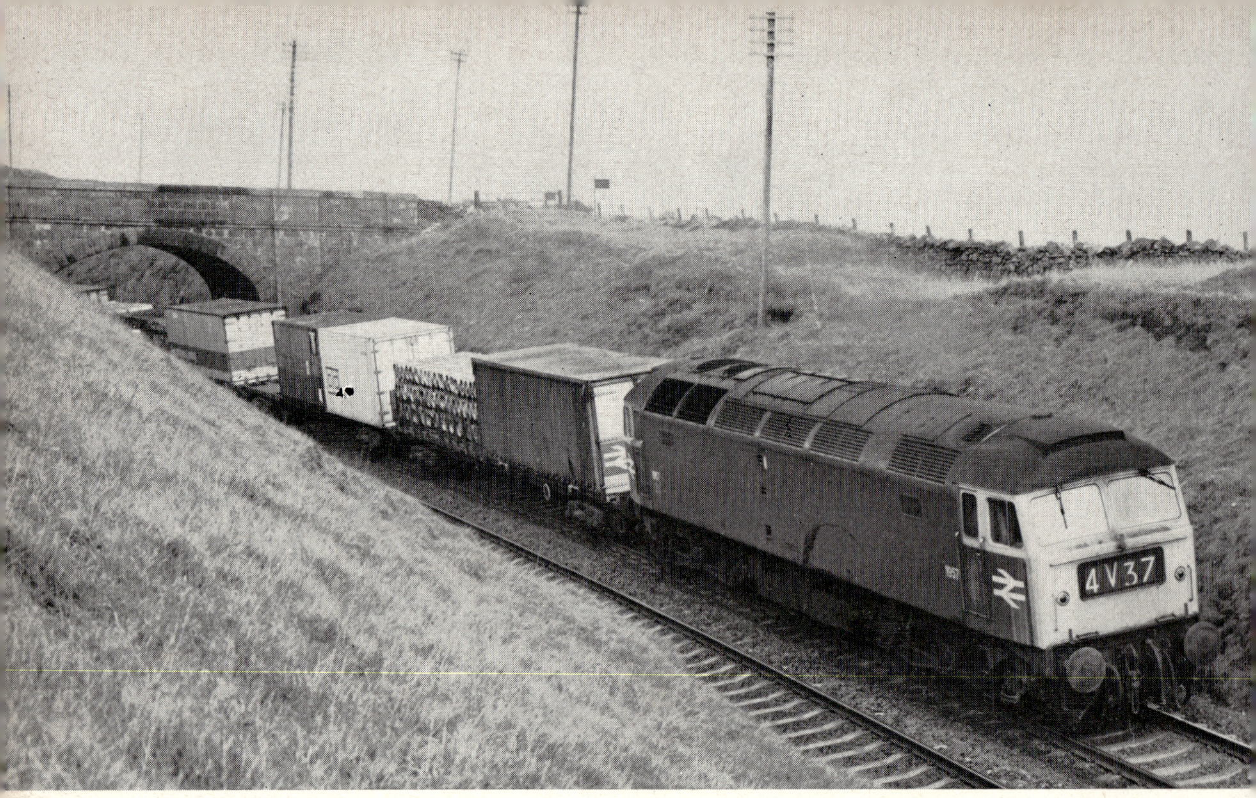
4V37

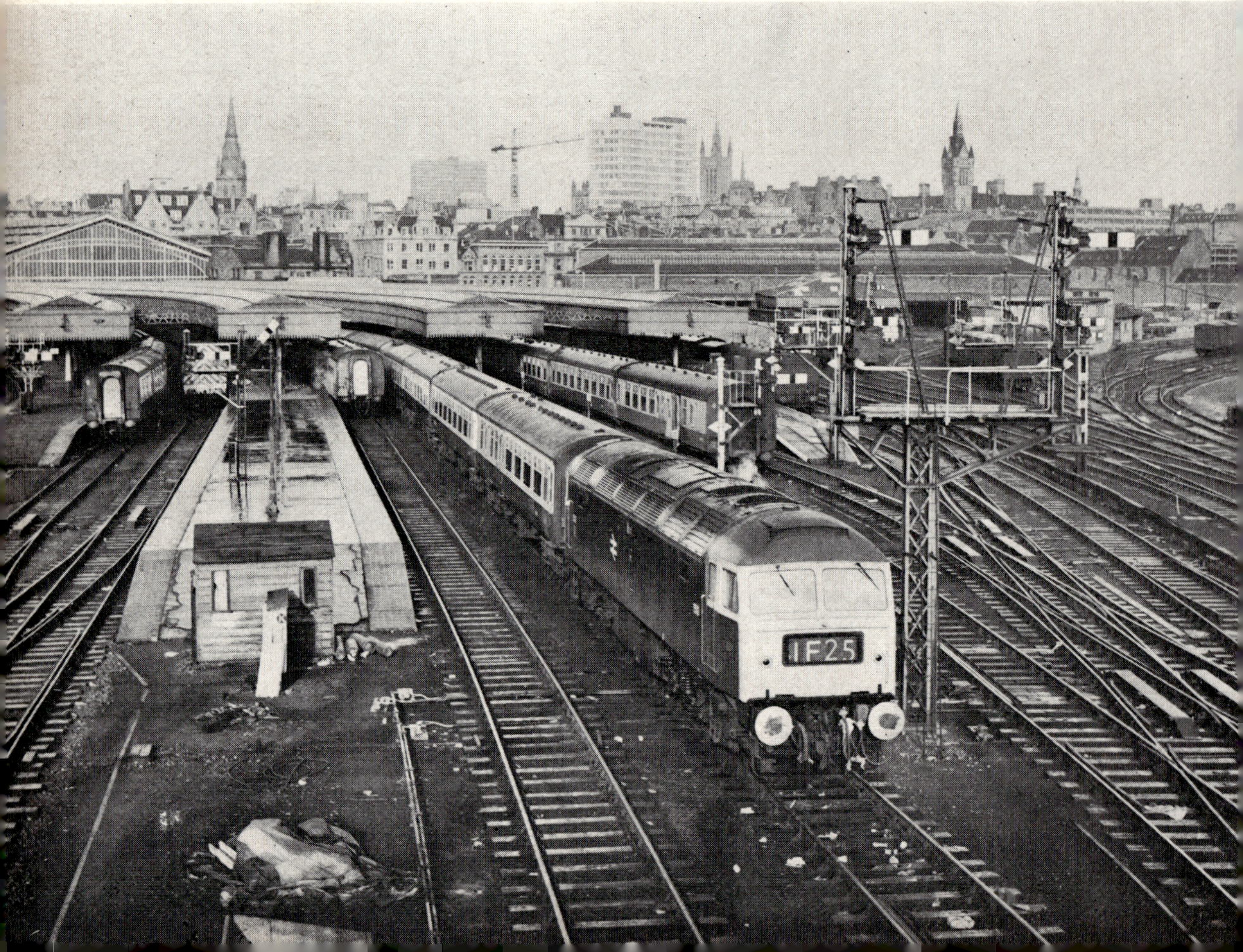
1F25

Left above: An up Freightliner near Cove Bay, Aberdeen, in March 1974 with Class 47/4 No 1957 (47.554) at the head. *Brian Morrison*

Left: Brush Class 47/4 No 1513 (47.414) leaving Aberdeen in November 1973 with the 12.20 (Sunday Aberdonian) to Kings Cross.
Brian Morrison

Above: Class 50 Co-Cos Nos 422 (50.022) and 428 (50.028) heading a down Royal Scot at Dumfries in July 1971. *Derek Cross*

Right: No 47.469 (1595) setting out from Carstairs for Edinburgh with the last four coaches of the 08.10 Birmingham-Glasgow/Edinburgh train in May 1974. *P. D. Hawkins*

Above: Class 50 No 413 (50.013) on a Sunday 11.55 Glasgow-Euston train in May 1973 approaching Rise Hill Tunnel. *J. H. Cooper-Smith*

Right above: Class 50 Nos 427 (50.027) and 402 (50.002) on a Sunday 11.55 Glasgow-Euston train in June 1972 approaching Birkett Tunnel.
J. H. Cooper-Smith

Right: Class 50 No 406 (50.006) passing Kingmoor Depot, Carlisle, with an up express in June 1973; Class 40 No 288 (40.088) is standing with a parcels train on the left. *C. R. Davis*

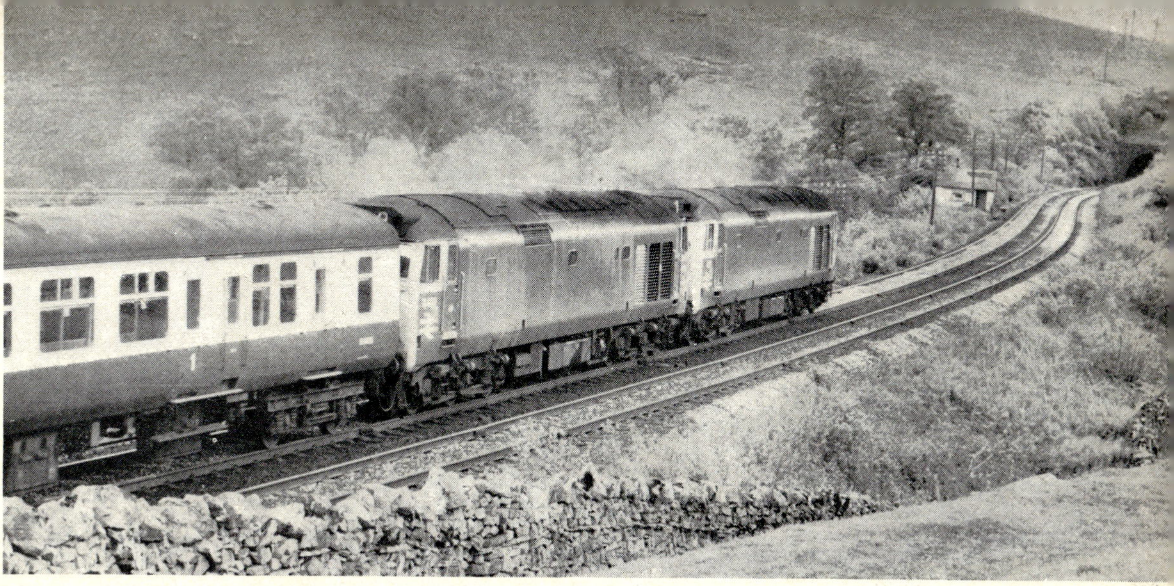

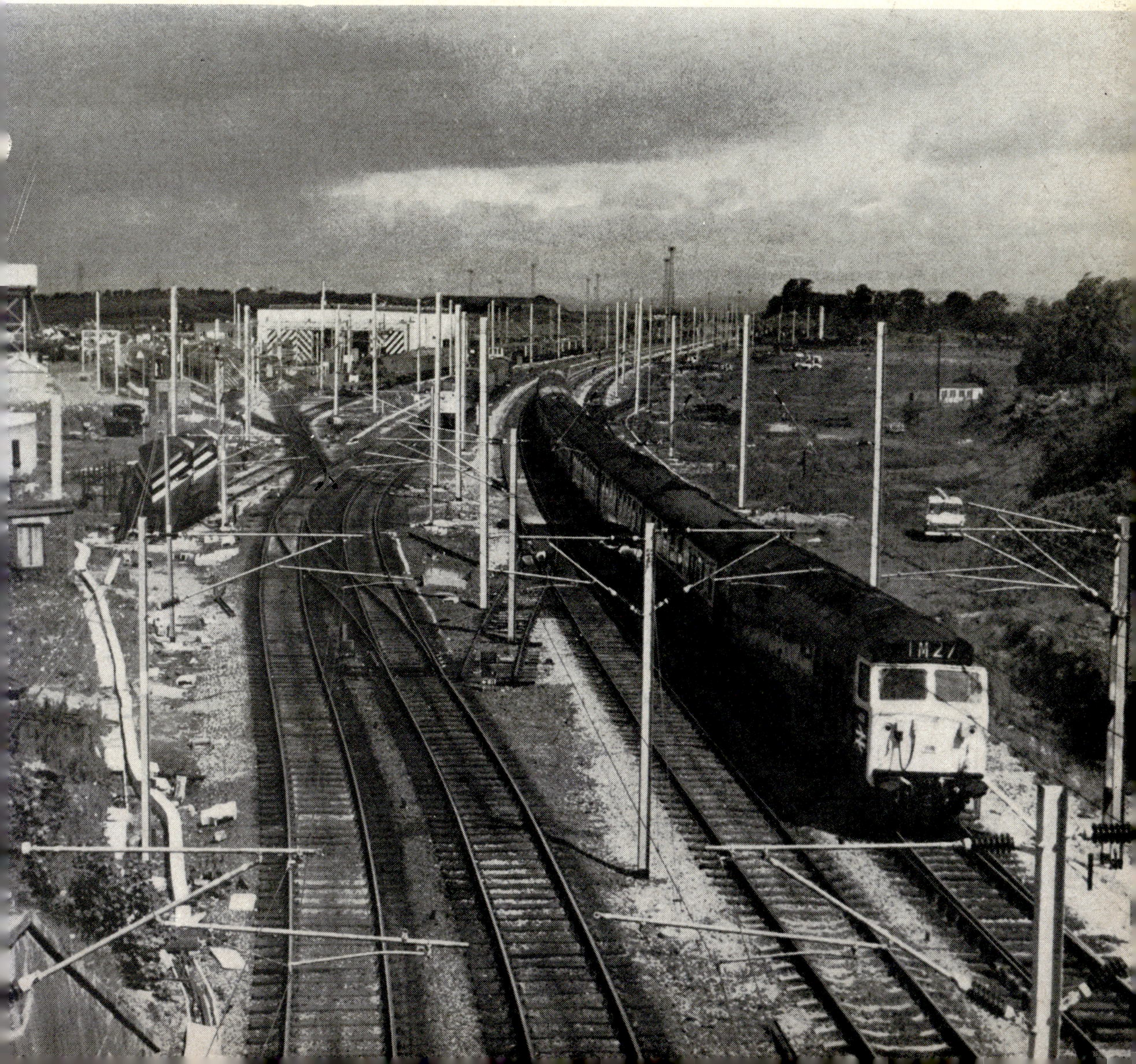
1M27

Above: Class 87 25kV ac 5000hp electric locomotive No 87.010 at the head of an Anglo-Scottish express awaits the right-away at Carstairs in June 1975.
F. R. Kerr

Right above: No 87.012 on a Glasgow-Birmingham train and a dmu for Kilmarnock at Glasgow Central in June 1975. *D. M. Cross*

Right: A Euston-Glasgow train rocketing up Shap behind No 87.025 in June 1974. *Brian Morrison*

Left: A pair of Class 76 1500V dc 1868hp electric locomotives about to enter Woodhead Tunnel with 30 loaded coal hoppers for Sheffield in July 1974.
P. D. Hawkins

Above: Nos 76.011 and 76.012 heading an empty merry-go-round coal train across Dinting Viaduct towards the Yorkshire coalfield in June 1975.
D. A. Flitcroft

Above: BR's prototype 125mph diesel-electric HST (high-speed train) arriving at Darlington on a demonstration run in August 1973. *M. Hall*

Left: Class 45 2500hp 1Co-Co1 No 75 on a Bristol-Newcastle train approaching Rotherham in May 1972.
J. H. Cooper-Smith

Right above: Class 55 3300hp Co-Co diesel-electric Deltic No 9013 (55.013) *The Black Watch* about to leave York on the 08.00 Kings Cross-Edinburgh train in September 1971. *J. H. Cooper-Smith*

Right: Deltic No 9004 (55.004) *Queen's Own Highlander* leaving Doncaster on the up Tees-Tyne Pullman in May 1970. *J. H. Cooper-Smith*

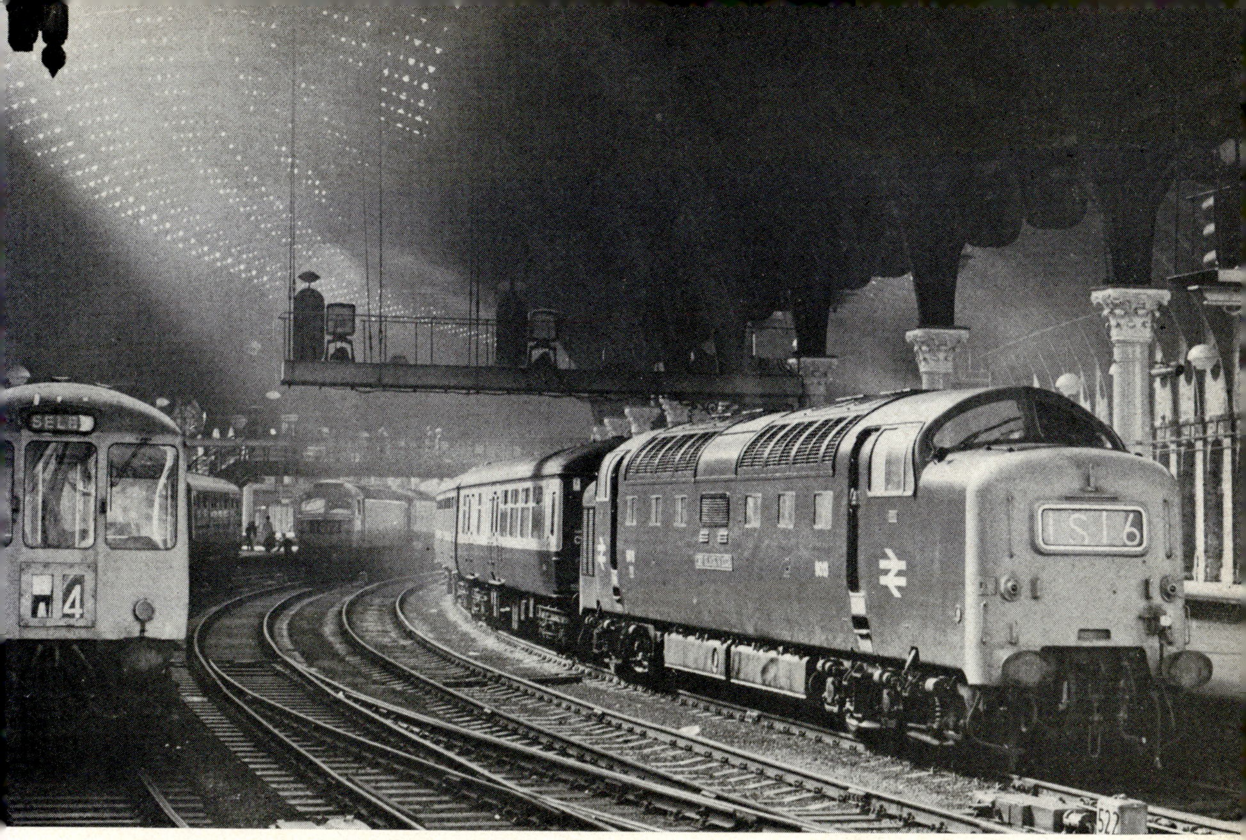
SELB
4
1S16

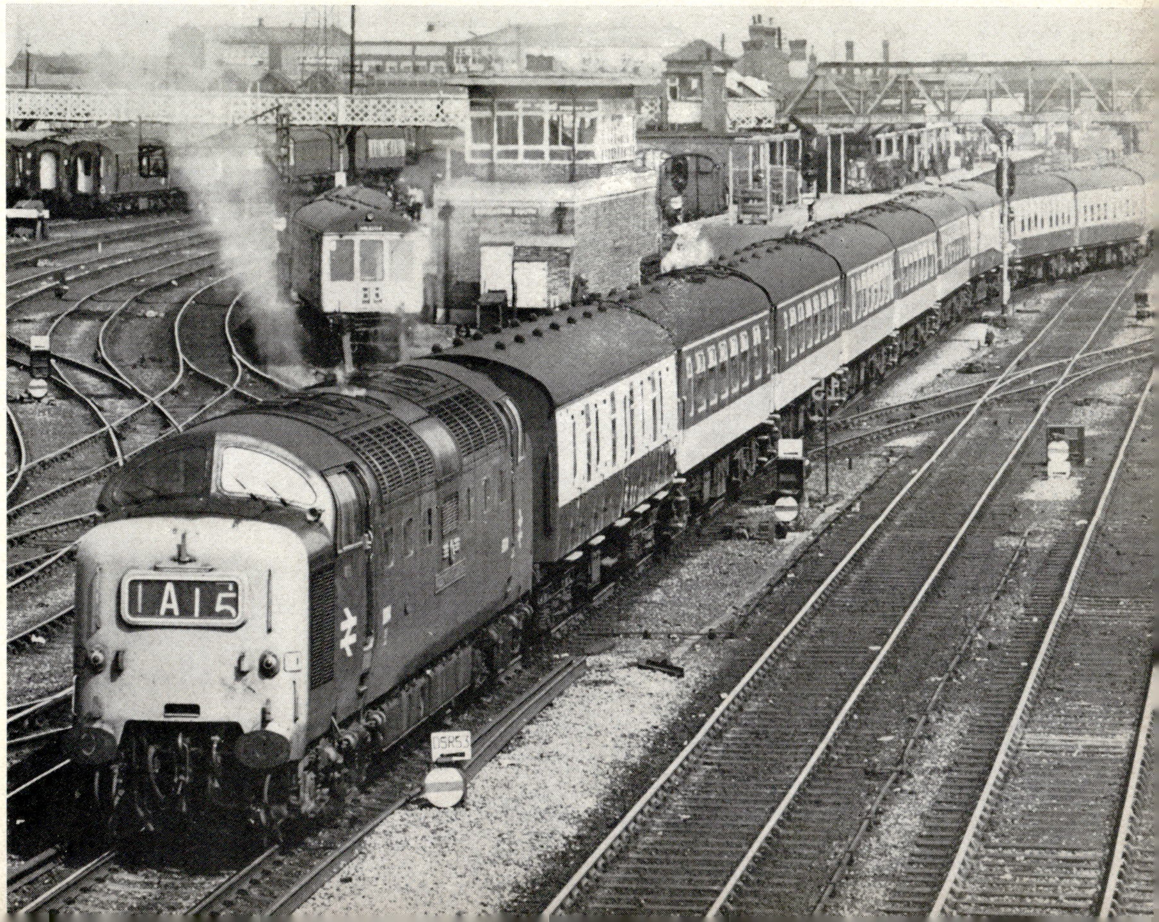
1A15

Left: A Bradford-Ilkley dmu leaving Shipley passing the grassed-over Shipley-Manningham goods lines (left) in April 1975. *B. A. Anderton*

Left centre: Gloucester RCW dmu at Reddish Station in September 1974. *B. J. Nicolle*

Left bottom: A trans-Pennine dmu working towards the Midland Region, standing at Leeds City Station in September 1974. *Kevin Lane*

Right: A Bury-Manchester emu leaving Bury in October 1974 about to cross the bridge over the Rochdale-Bury-Bolton line trackbed. *D. A. Flitcroft*

Below: A Manchester-Southport dmu approaching Wigan in March 1971. *J. H. Cooper-Smith*

TOTLEY TUNNEL

Left above: Preserved LNER Gresley 2-6-2 No 4771 *Green Arrow* heading the Red Rose excursion towards Carnforth in September 1974. *T. G. Flinders*

Left: Streamlined A4 Pacific No 4498 *Sir Nigel Gresley* approaching Haltwhistle on a Newcastle-Carlisle steam safari in June 1972. *G. R. Hounsell*

Above: One of the preserved LMS Stanier 4-6-0s, No 5596 *Bahamas* leaving Totley Tunnel at Grindleford in June 1973. *J. H. Cooper-Smith*

27

Left above: Great Western Society's 4-6-0 No 6998 *Burton Agnes Hall* climbing towards Culham with the William Shakespeare tour in September 1973.

T. G. Flinders

Left: Another GW Society preservation, 2-6-2T No 6106 leading No 6998 on a Didcot-Didcot via Oxford test run in July 1973. *D. E. Canning*

Above: David Shepherd's BR 2-10-0 No 92203 *Black Prince* at Alderbury, south of Salisbury, on its way to Westbury from Eastleigh in April 1975.

R. E. B. Siviter

29

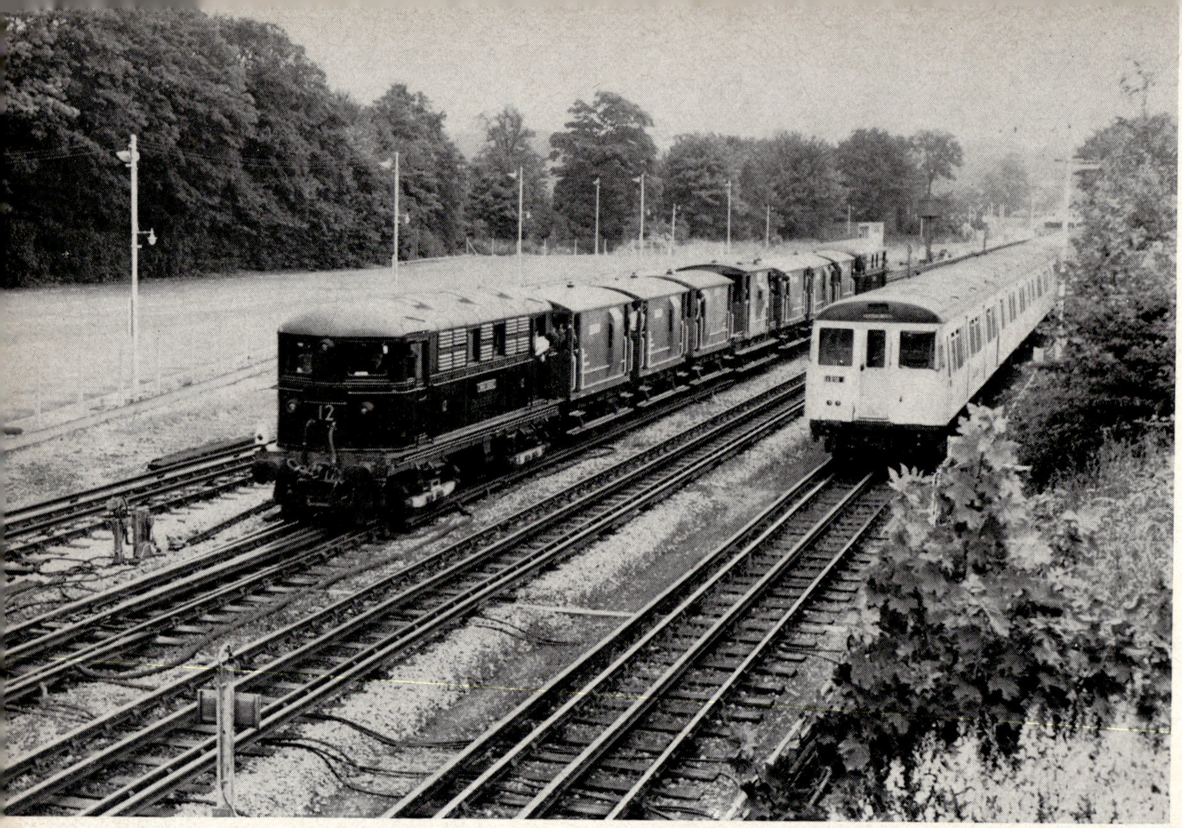

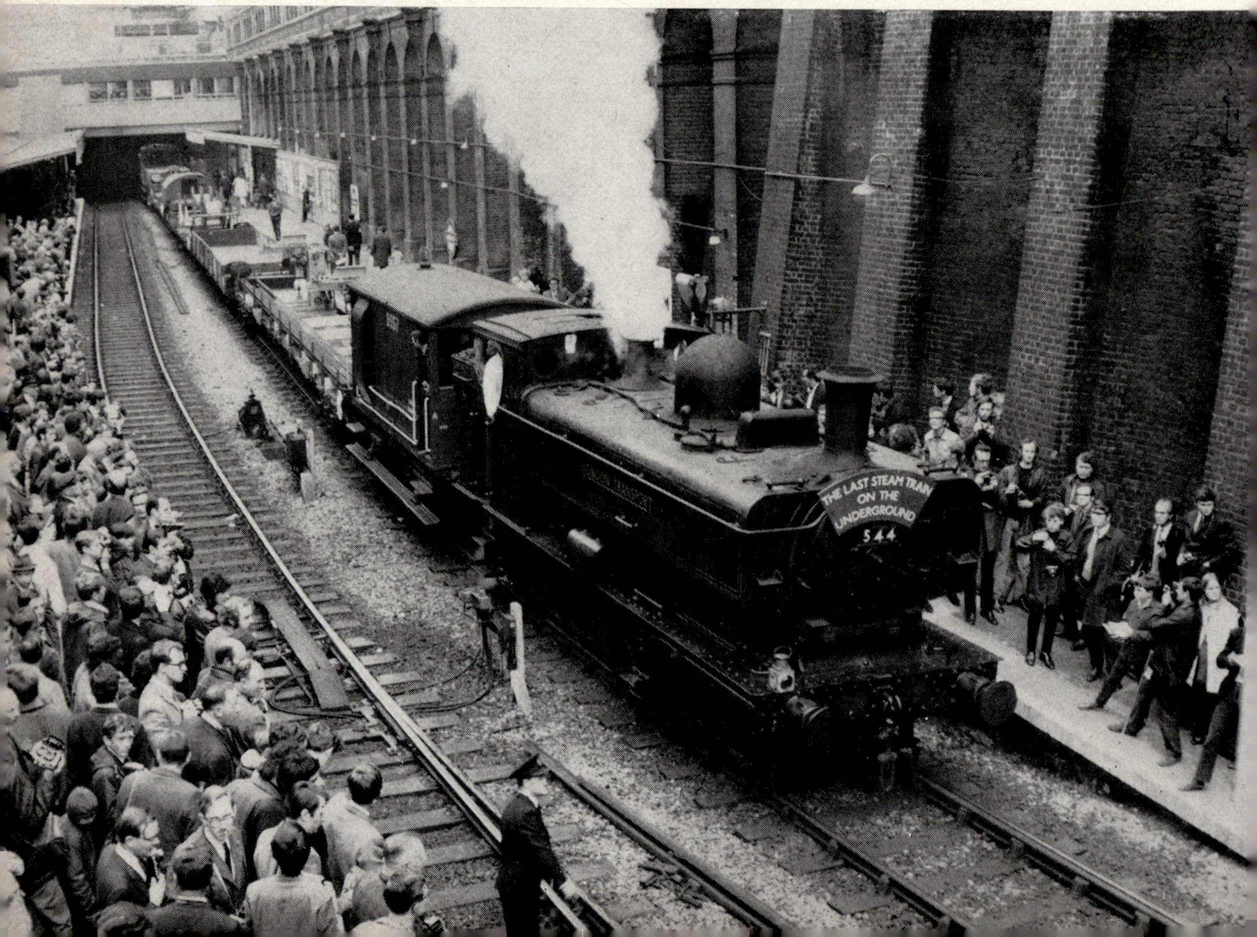

THE LAST STEAM TRAIN ON THE UNDERGROUND 544

Left above: London Transport Metropolitan Electrics Railtour passing Rickmansworth in July 1972.
G. D. King

Left: Ceremonial last steam train on London's Underground hauled by ex-GWR 0-6-0PT pauses at Barbican Station in June 1971 for photographers.
Garry Merrin

Above: A Bakerloo Line train leaving Queens Park Depot in April 1970.
A. W. Hobson

Right: Richmond and Edgware trains of LT R stock passing at Earls Court Station in February 1974. *Kevin Lane*

Above: The HST on the 13.45 Bristol-Paddington train near Corsham in May 1975. *J. H. Cooper-Smith*

Right: The HST getting ready to leave Paddington Station in July 1975. *G. F. Scott-Lowe*

33

Above: Swindon Inter-City dmu No L706 on an up excursion train in Sonning Cutting in April 1974.
Brian Morrison

Right: Class 46 No 46.025 (162) passing the Bromsgrove platform at the foot of the Lickey Bank with the southbound Leeds-Paignton Devonian in February 1974. *P. D. Hawkins*

Right above: Class 52 No 1067 *Western Druid* pulls out of Solihull with a Birmingham-Paddington train in May 1975. *P. D. Hawkins*

Left: At Kidsgrove in April 1975, Class 304/1 emus No 003 (on left) leaves with a Stoke-on-Trent and Manchester train and No 010 arrives with a Manchester-Stafford train.
P. D. Hawkins

Above: A selection of electric and diesel units (Classes 85, 87 and 50) at Crewe diesel depot in February 1975.
D. N. Clough

Right: A Derby-built three-car dmu forming the 15.10 Moor Street-Henley-in-Arden train at Birmingham Moor Street in September 1974.
P. D. Hawkins

Above: A cross-London goods train approaching Hither Green behind EE Co-Co 1750hp Class 37 No 37.059 (6759) in August 1975. *Kevin Lane*

Left: A BRCW Class 33 Bo-Bo 1550hp diesel-electric locomotive on a Dover-West Kensington train of coal empties at Elmstead Woods in May 1974. *Brian Morrison*

Right above: Class 33/2 No 33.205 (6590) with a Blue Circle Cement train near Petts Wood in August 1974. *Brian Morrison*

Right: Class 47 No 47.004 (1524) with a SR to ER transfer freight for West London lines at Clapham Cutting in September 1974. *Brian Morrison*

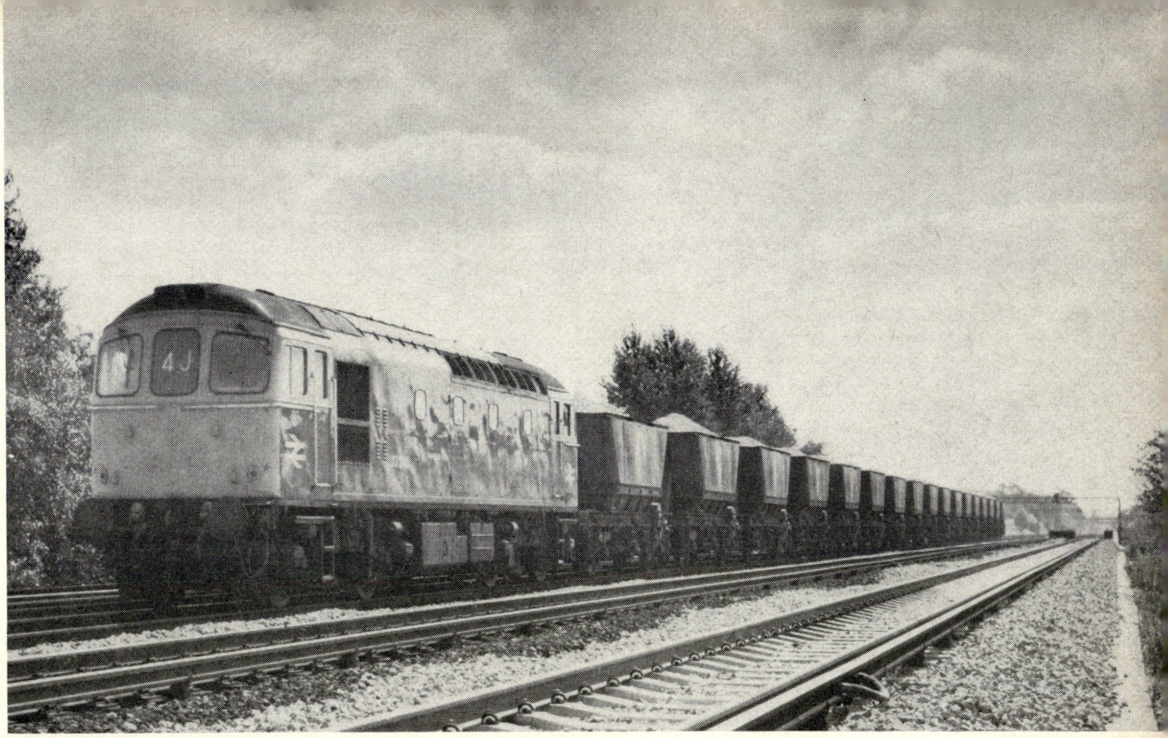
4J

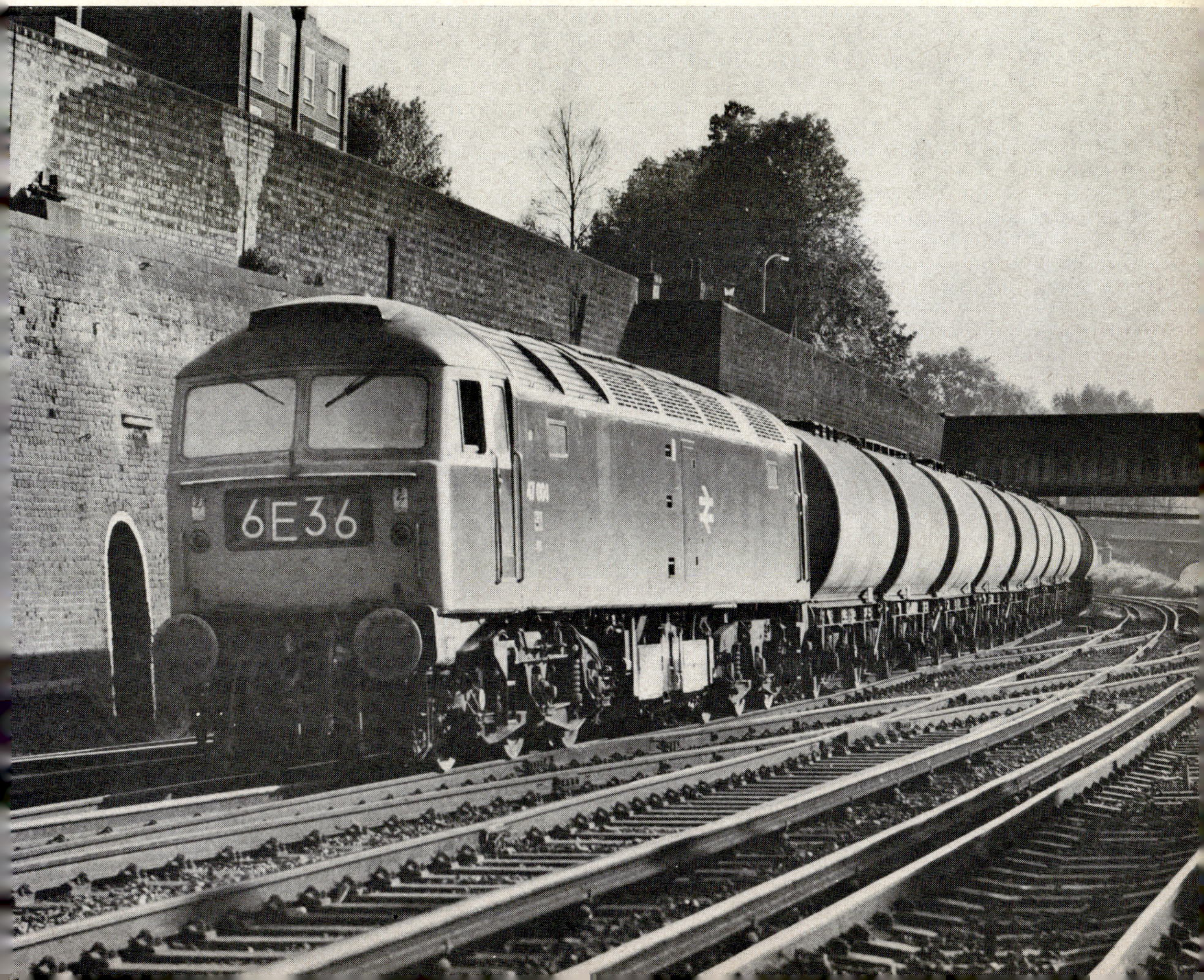
6E36

Above: Class 71 750V dc Bo-Bo electric locomotive No 71.002 (E5002) heading a scrap-iron transfer from Eastern Region for Dover, approaching St Mary Cray in August 1974. *Brian Morrison*

Right above: A Class 73 1600/600hp electro-diesel locomotive heading an oil train along the Kent coast past Margate in May 1970. *David Birch*

Right: A Class 35 heading an Amalgamated Roadstone Corporation aggregates train at Maidstone in November 1971. *British Rail*

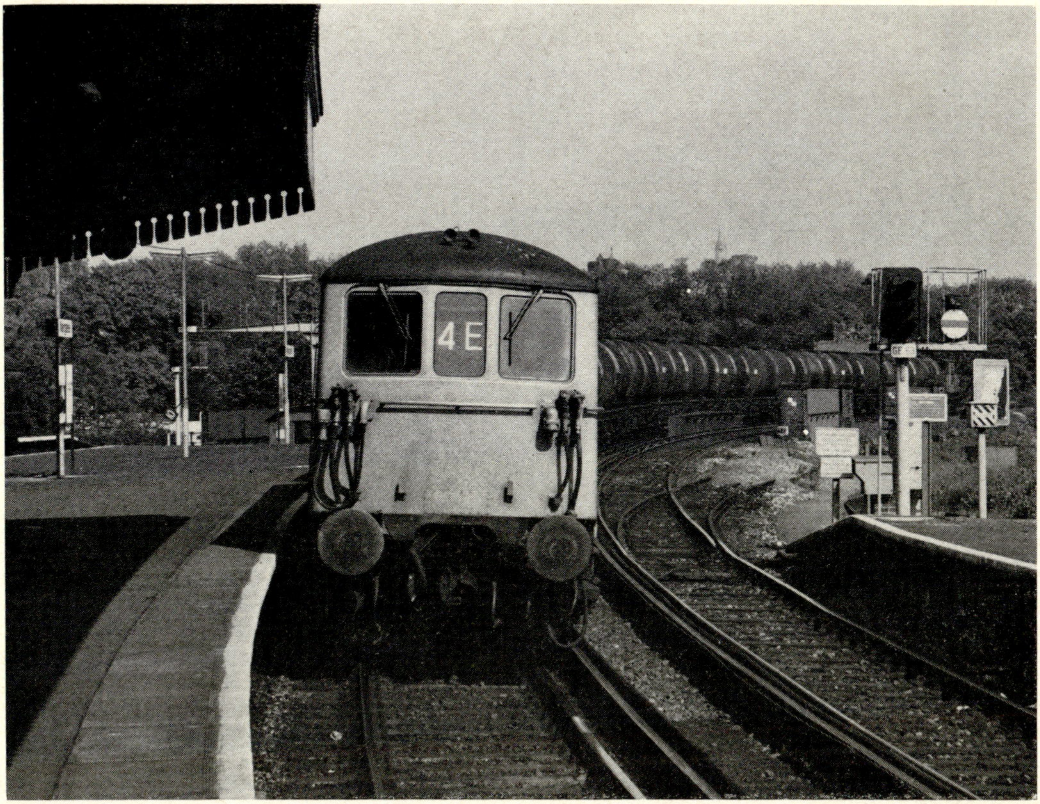
4E

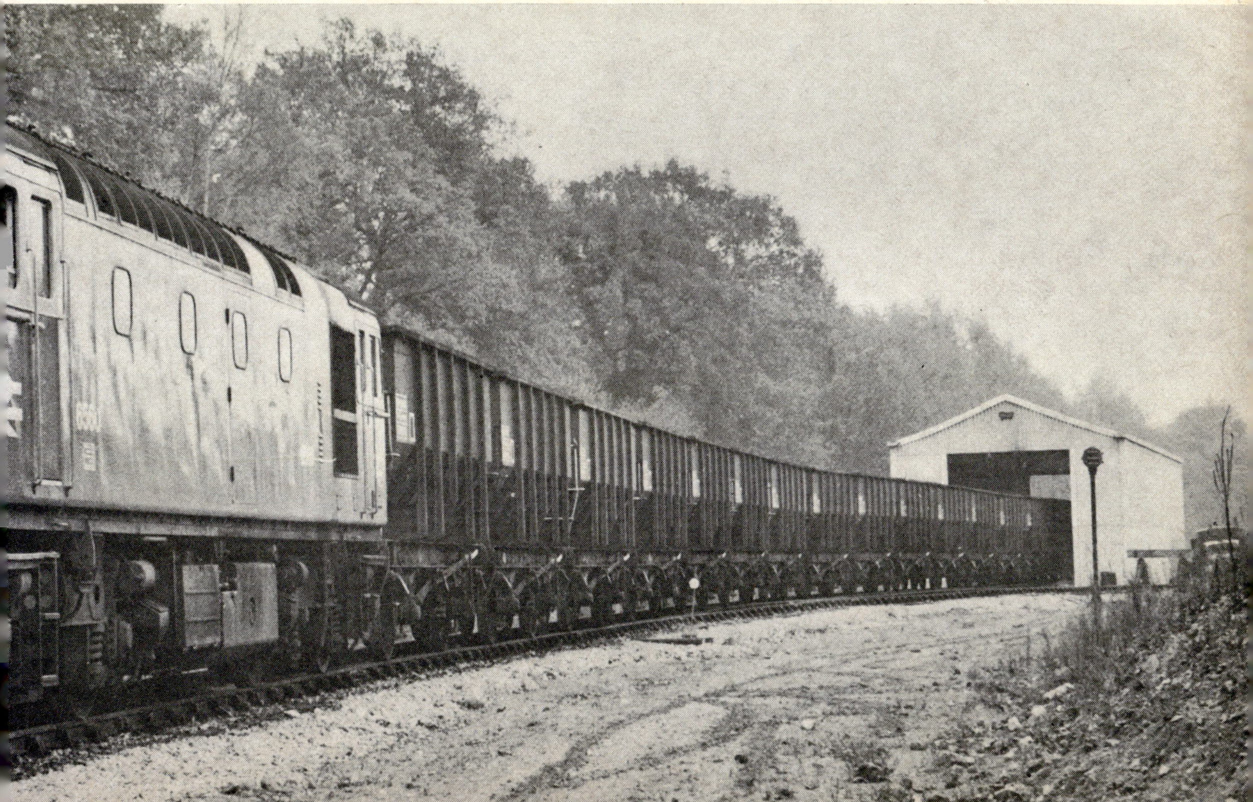

Right: A train of 2HAP emus heading south through Brixton Station in August 1975. *Kevin Lane*

Below: A 4EPB unit on a Charing Cross-Bexley Heath-Dartford service at London Bridge in July 1975.
Graham B. Wise

Far right: Two 4CEP units and one 4BEP forming a Dover Marine-Victoria train between St Mary Cray and Bickley in August 1974.
Brian Morrison

Far right below:
A Hastings-Charing Cross train formed of SR demus climbing Hildenborough bank in May 1973. *Brian Morrison*

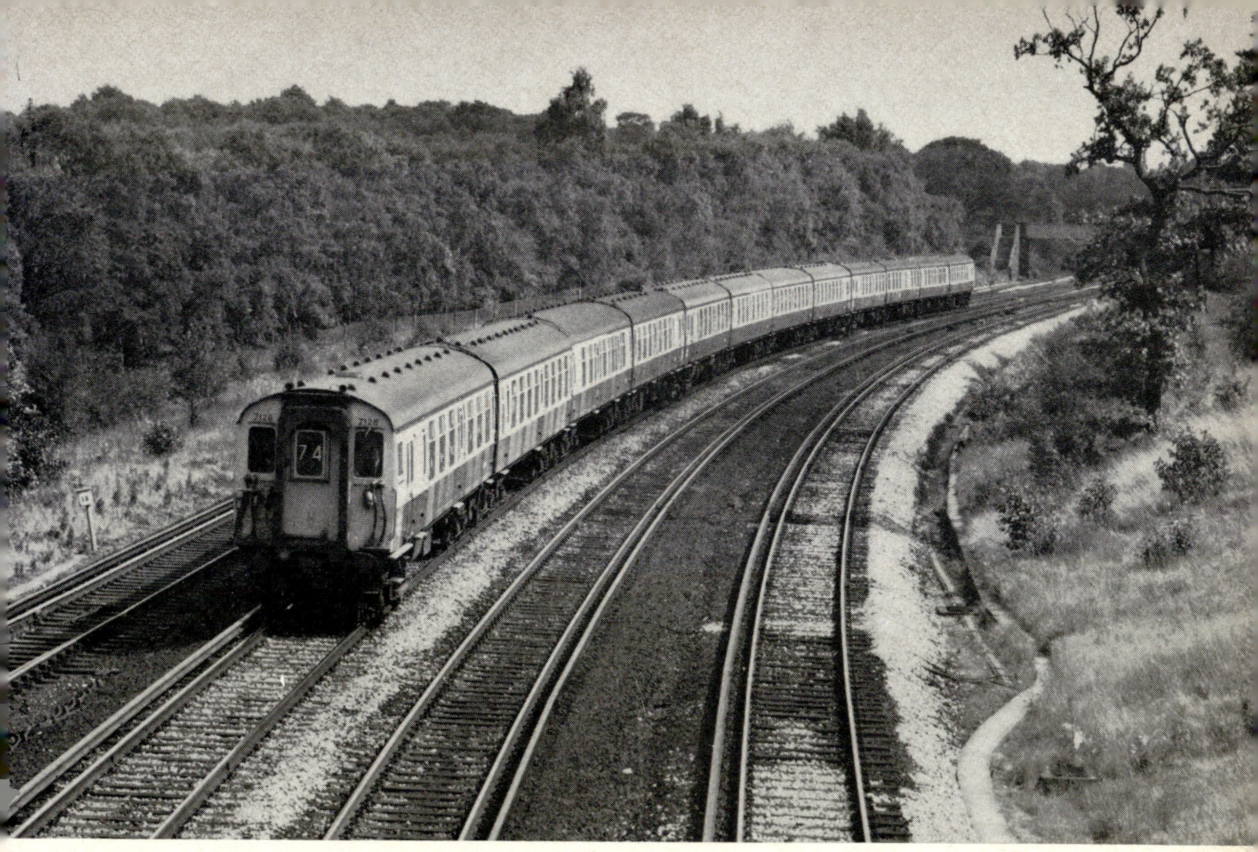
74

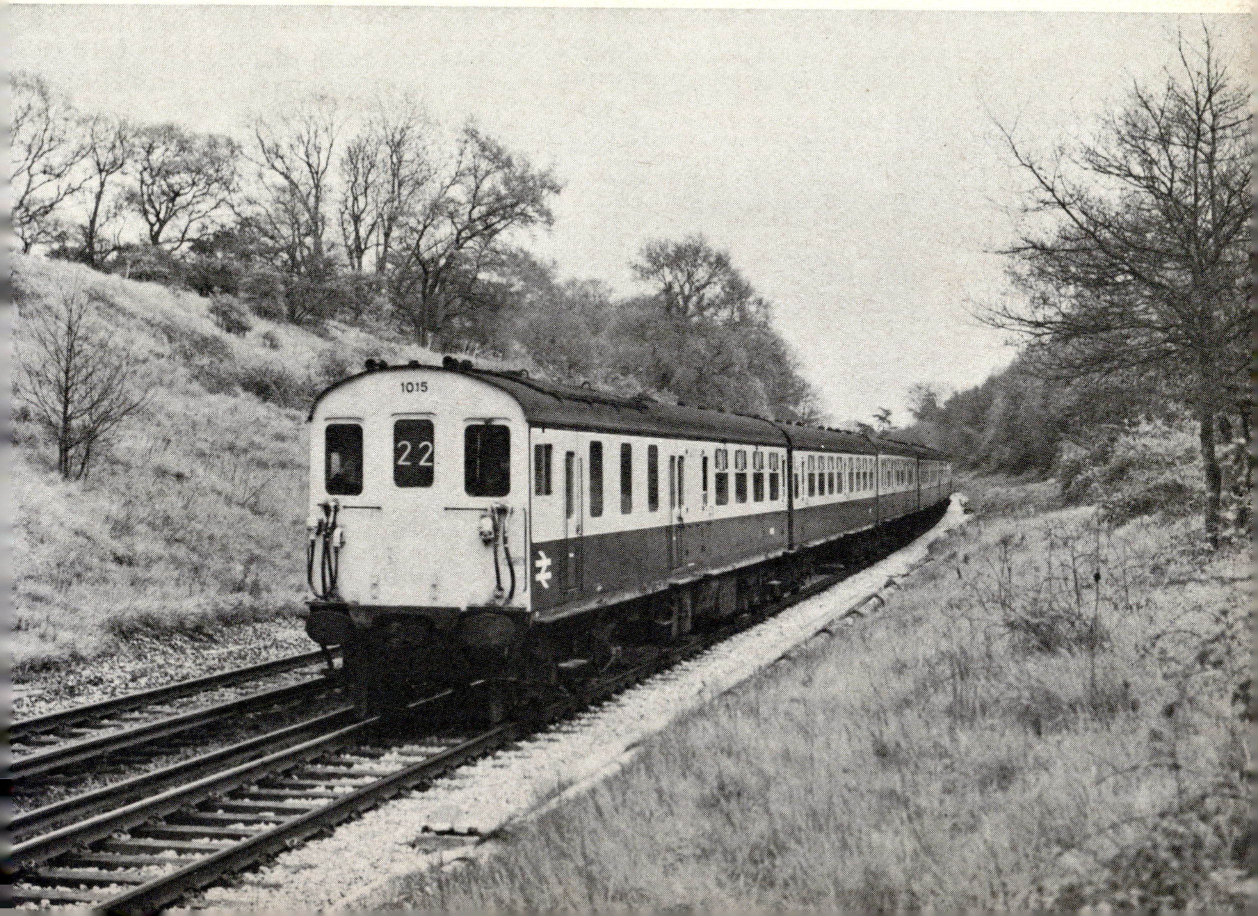
1015
22

Above: Prototype 4PEP high-density units approaching Clapham Junction with a Shepperton-Waterloo train in August 1975. *Kevin Lane*

Below: A 10-car formation of 2HAPs on a Charing Cross-Sevenoaks train leaving Elmstead Woods in August 1974. *Brian Morrison*

Left: Class 73 electro-diesel locomotive E6031 (73.124) and coach forming a guards' route knowledge special at Horsham in May 1973.   *J. Scrace*

Below: The Weymouth portion of a train from Waterloo leaving Dorchester behind Class 33 diesel-electric No 33.119 (6580) in April 1975.   *G. F. Gillham*

Right: A Dover-Charing Cross train of 4CEPs at Folkestone Warren in July 1971.   *J. H. Cooper-Smith*

Left: Three-car 3R 'tadpole' demu on a Reading-Tonbridge service at Chilworth & Albury in February 1974.
J. H. Cooper-Smith

Above & right: Ex-London Transport stock, now BR 3TIS three-car emus for Isle of Wight services, at Ryde Esplanade in July 1974 *(above, R. A. King)* and at Ryde Pierhead in September 1974.
R. I. Wallace

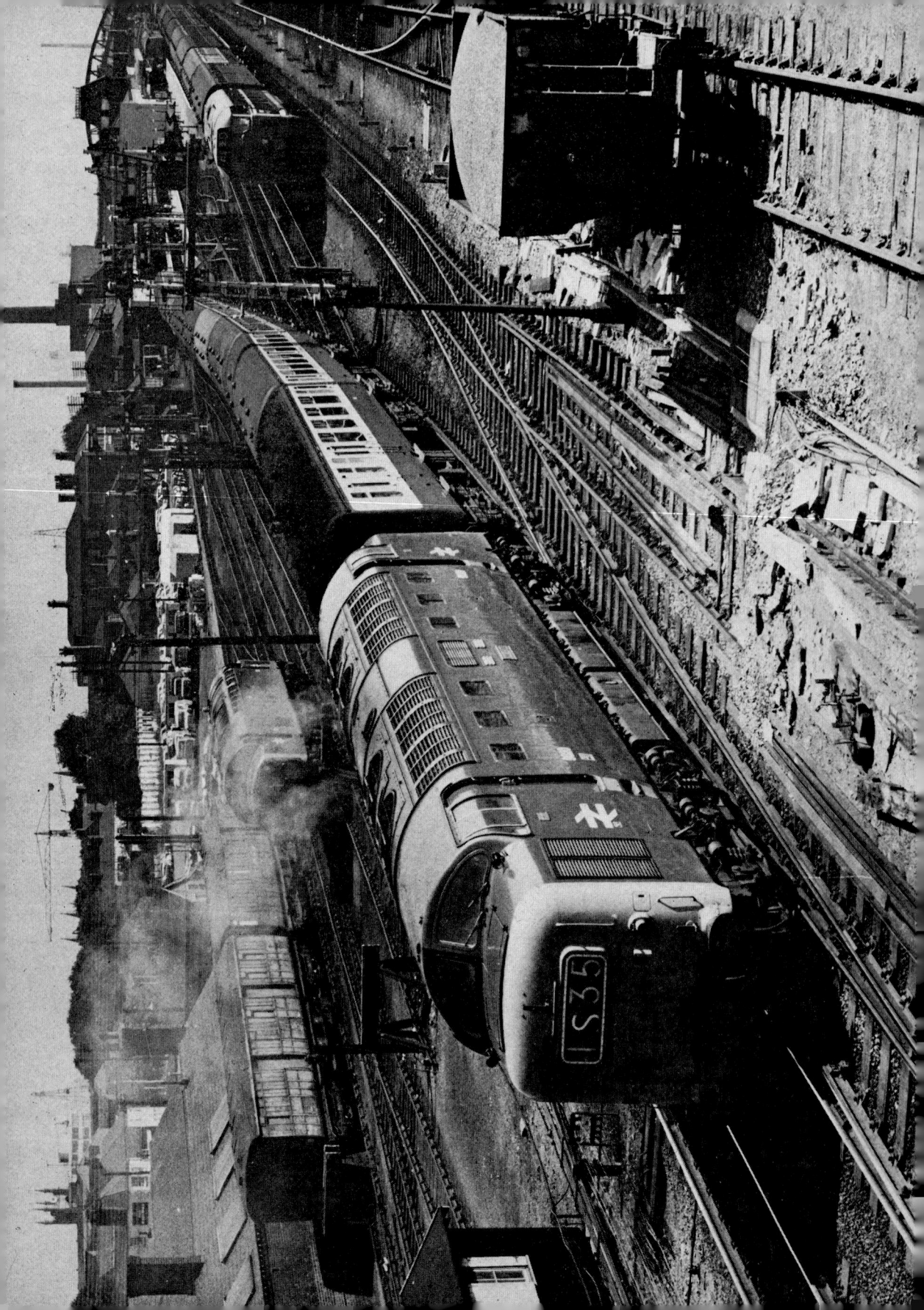

Left: Deltic No 9020 (55.020) *Nimbus* on a Kings Cross-Edinburgh train, leaving Peterborough in July 1970.   *J. H. Cooper-Smith*

Above: Up Flying Scotsman in May 1973 taking the new high-speed track through Peterborough, which raised permitted speed there from 20 to 100mph.

British Rail

Below: Class 25 1250hp Bo-Bo diesel-electrics Nos 25.044 (5194) and 25.064 (5214) arriving at Lincoln Central with a Manchester-Yarmouth train in June 1975.   *Graham B. Wise*

Right: A Tilbury-Garston Freightliner headed by Class 47 No 1522 (47.002) between Pinfleet and Rainham in March 1973. *Brian Morrison*

Below: A Leeds-Parkeston Freightliner behind unidentified diesel making steady progress up Belstead Bank, Ipswich, at about the turn of the decade.
G. R. Mortimer

Right below: Felixstowe Dock & Railway Co's Freightliner terminal in November 1972 soon after its opening. *Port of Felixstowe*

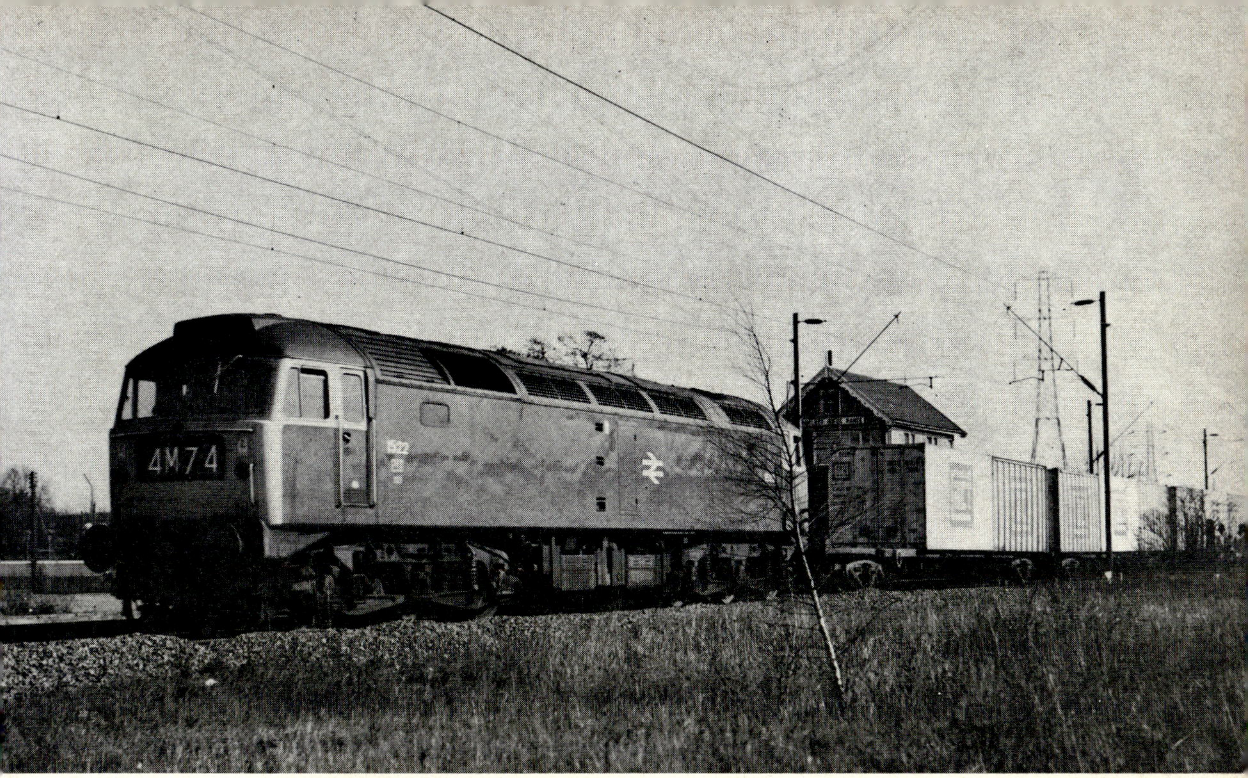
4M74

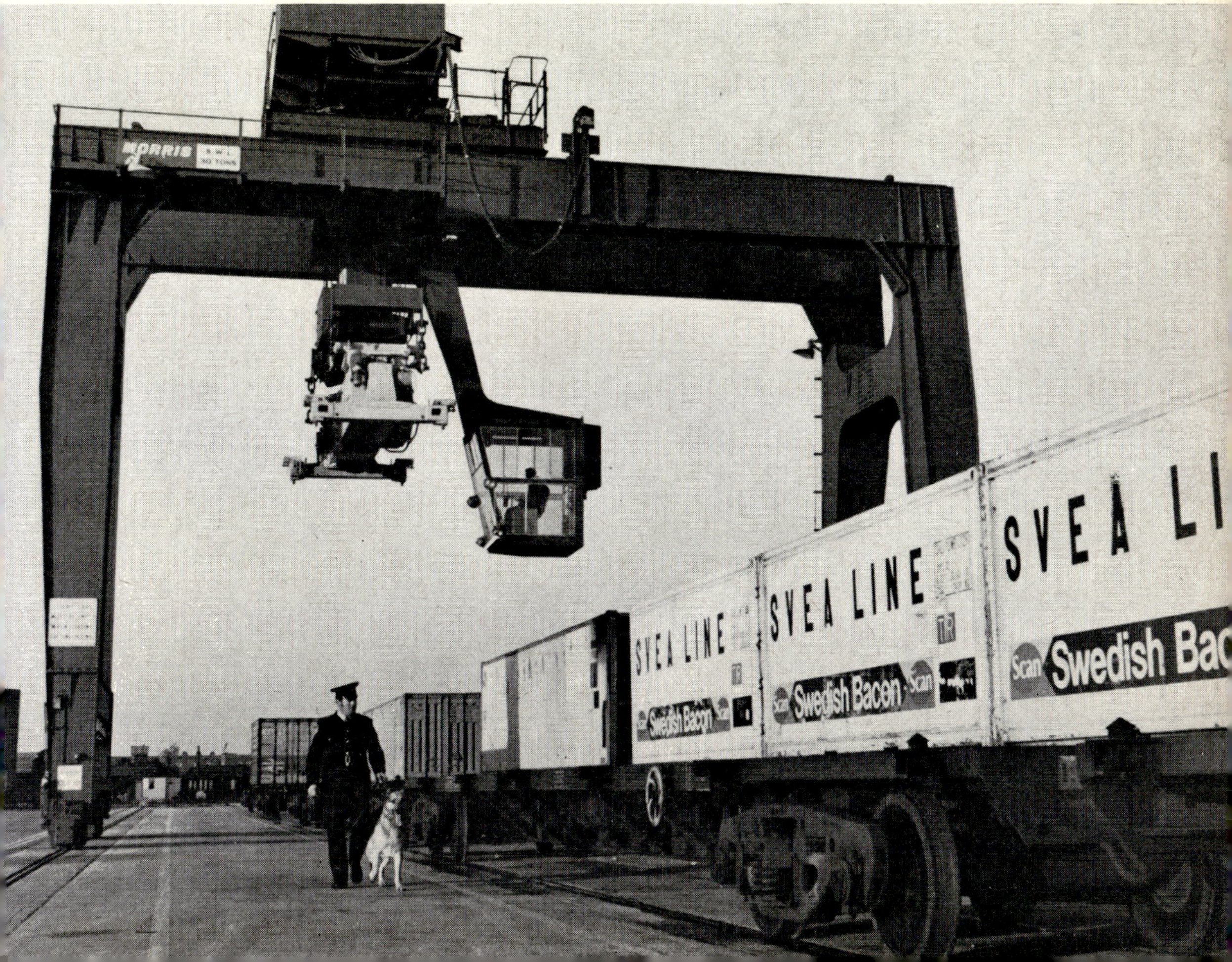
MORRIS
SVEA LINE
Swedish Bacon
Scan

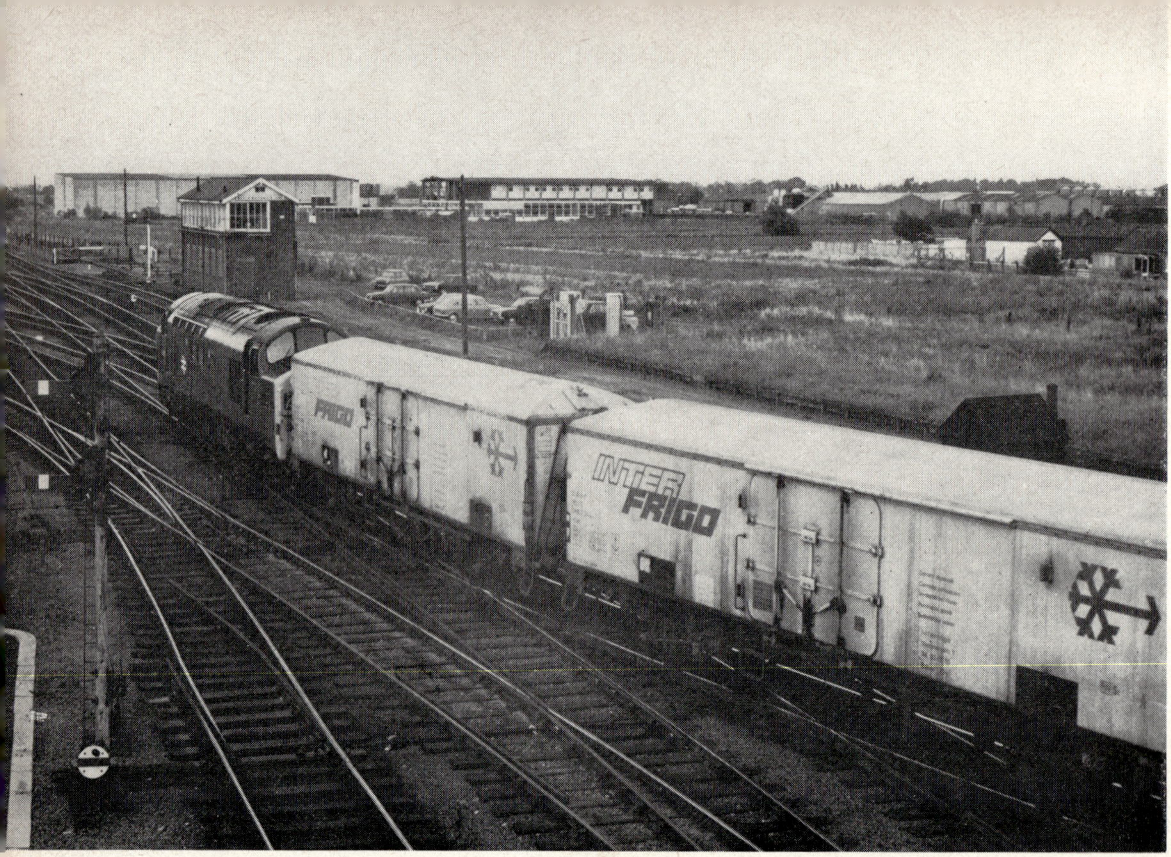
FRIGO
INTER
FRIGO

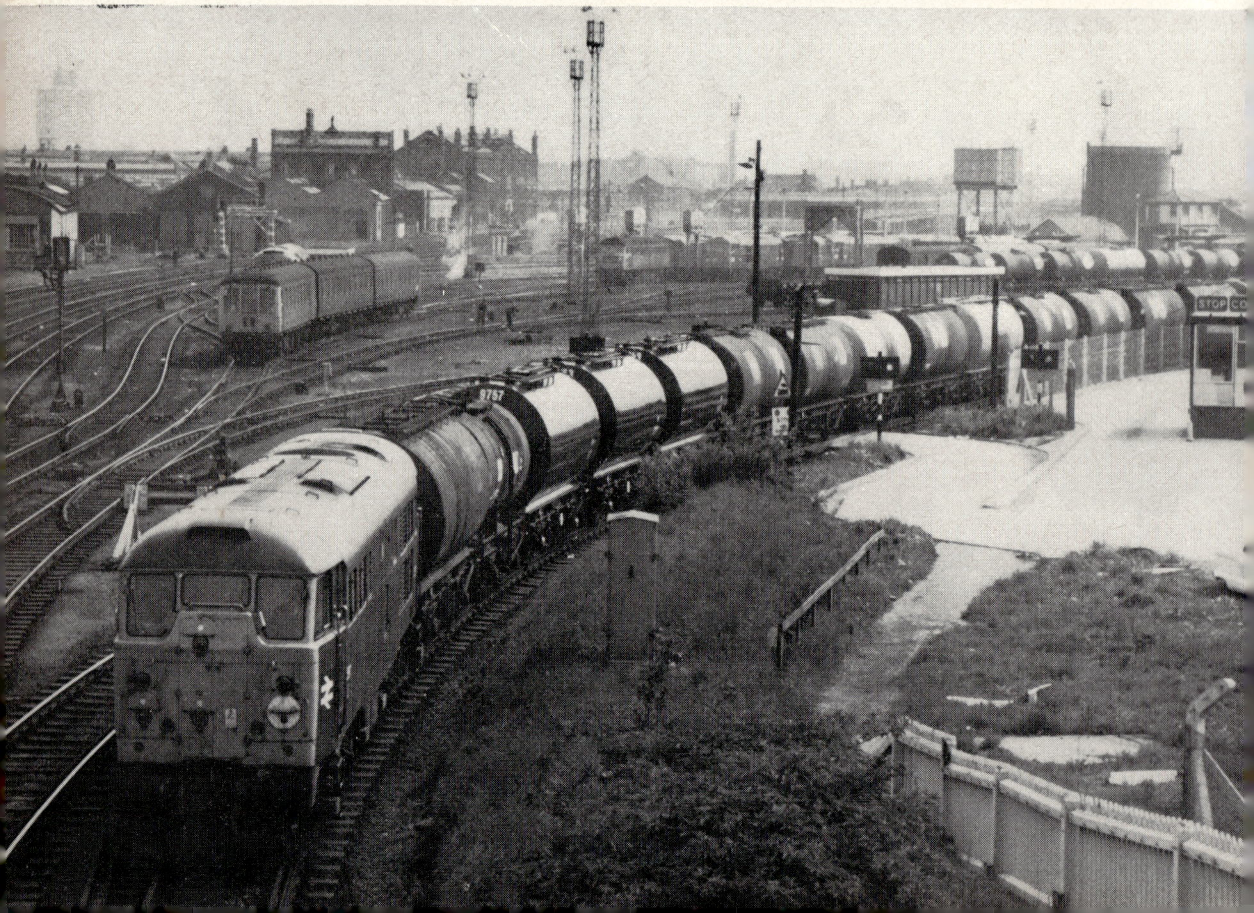
STOP

Left above: Class 37 with European Interfrigo vans in train passing March Whitemoor Junction in September 1974. *B. G. Barrett*

Above: Class 37 No 6750 (37.050) leaving Dagenham with a westbound Ford Company train in May 1973. *J. H. Cooper-Smith*

Left: Class 31 No 5507 (31.007) heading an oil train into Temple Mills from the North London spur at Stratford at around the turn of the decade.
J. H. Cooper-Smith

Left above: A Cambridge-Channelsea Carriage Sidings parcels train at Littlebury headed by Class 31/1 No 5518 (31.101) in June 1973. *G. R. Mortimer*

Left: Two Class 25s at Whitwood heading a Rylstone Hull Tilcon train, showing a wrong headcode incidentally. *J. G. Glover*

Above: A Class 03 204hp 0-6-0 diesel-mechanical shunter at work on one of the few remaining sections of the M&GN track, on the site of demolished South Lynn Station, in August 1974. The bridge has since been removed for road works and a new bridge provides rail access to a sugar beet factory. *R. A. King*

57

Left: Mixed dmu cars, a Metro-Cammell unit leading, forming a Doncaster-Cambridge train on the March curve out of Spalding in April 1975.
Graham B. Wise

Below: A St Ives-Cambridge train at Long Stanton during the last week of passenger service on the GE St Ives branch in October 1970.
G. R. Mortimer

Right: Class 31/1 No 31.160 (5578) heads a special run to mark the reopening of Magdalen Road Station on the Great Eastern on May 5, 1975.
G. R. Mortimer

Left: A Metro-Cammell dmu forming a Doncaster-Ely service at Greetwell Junction on the GN-GE joint line in May 1974. *Graham B. Wise*

Below: Class 47/4 No 47.524 (1107) with a Kings Cross-Grimsby and Cleethorpes train rounding the curve out of Lincoln St Marks in April 1975.
Graham B. Wise

Right: LTE District Line train out east, entering Upminster Station from the sidings to start service to Ealing Broadway in August 1973.
Brian Morrison

Below: BR Class 306 emu on Gidea Park-Liverpool Street service at Chadwell Heath in July 1975. *Kevin Lane*

Left: Great Eastern Class N7 0-6-2T of the Stour Valley Railway Preservation Society at Chappel & Wakes Colne Station in September 1973.
G. R. Mortimer

Below: North Norfolk Railway's Kitson *Colwyn* and Peckett No 1970, both 0-6-0STs, heading a special bound for Weybourne at Sheringham on a members' open day for the Midland & Great Northern Joint Railway Society in May 1974. *Brian Fisher*

Right: A closer look at *Colwyn*, Kitson's No 5470 of 1933, this time on a works train from Sheringham to Weybourne in July 1975.
W. R. Squires

Right below: Colne Valley Railway Society's ex-WD 0-6-0ST No 190 in steam near Castle Hedingham in March 1975, marking the 10th anniversary of closure of the line. *John D. Mann*

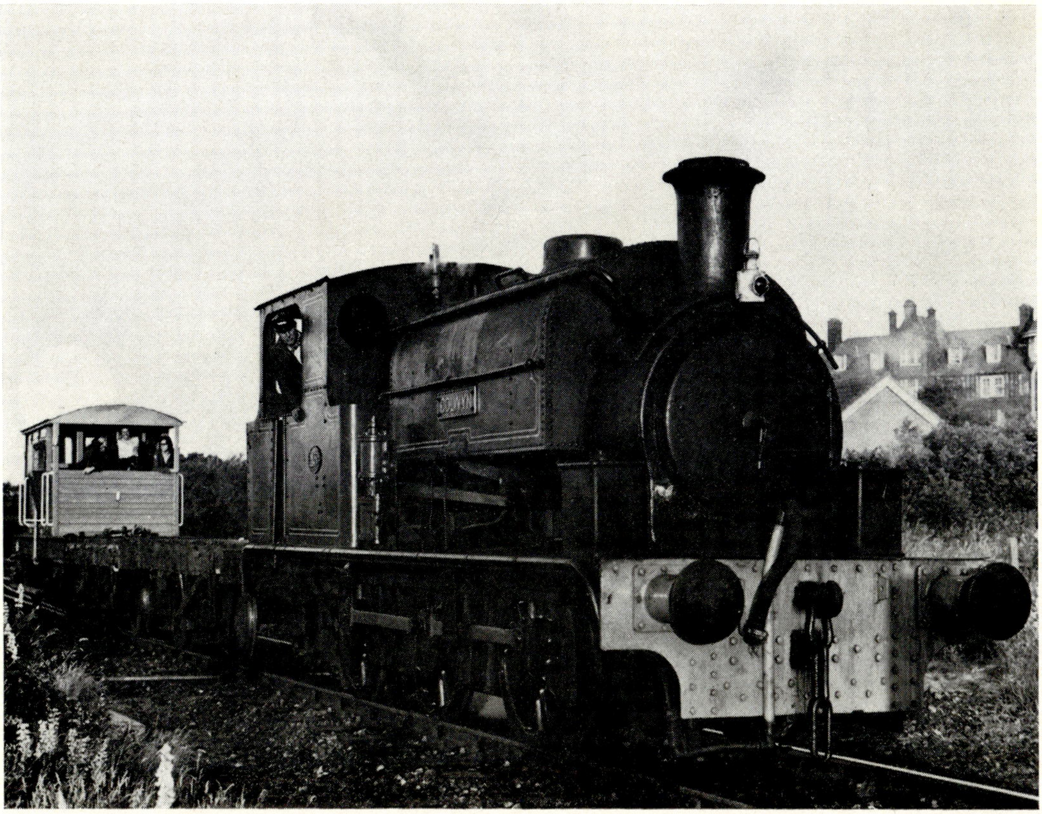

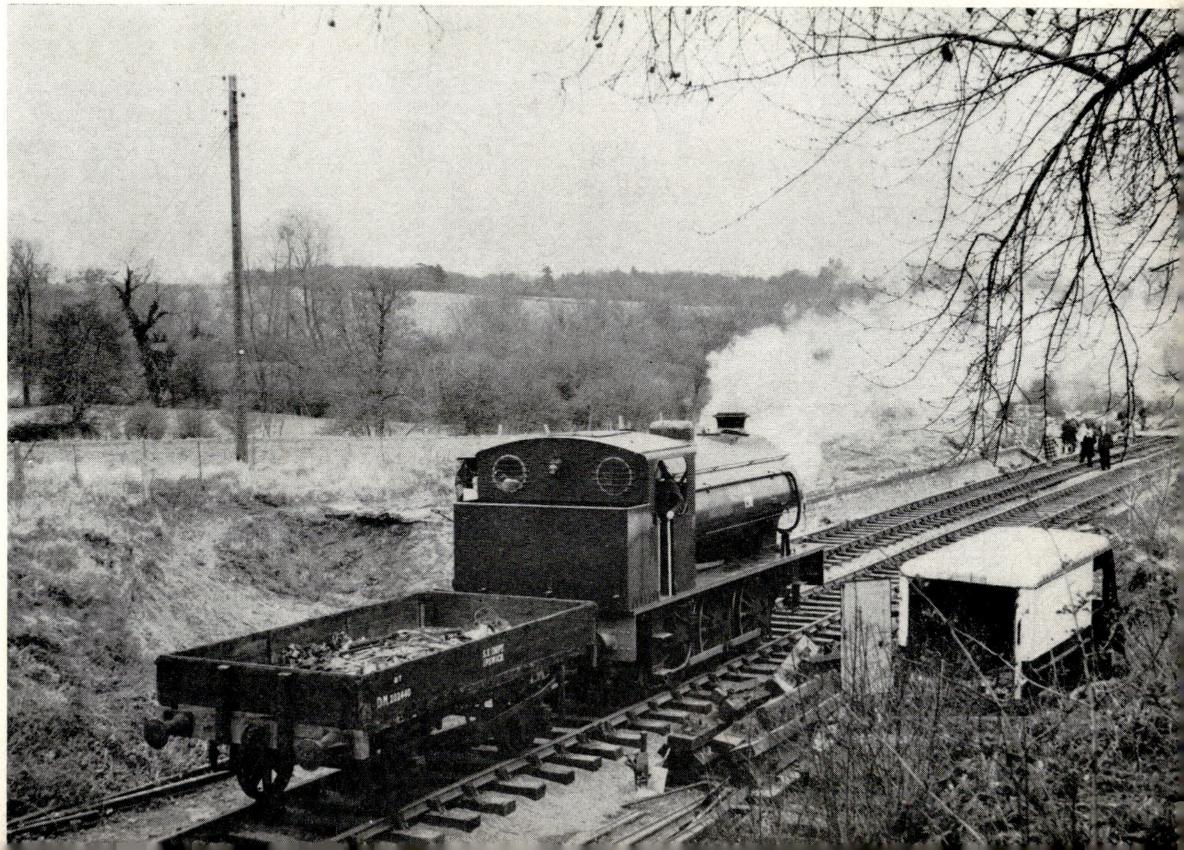

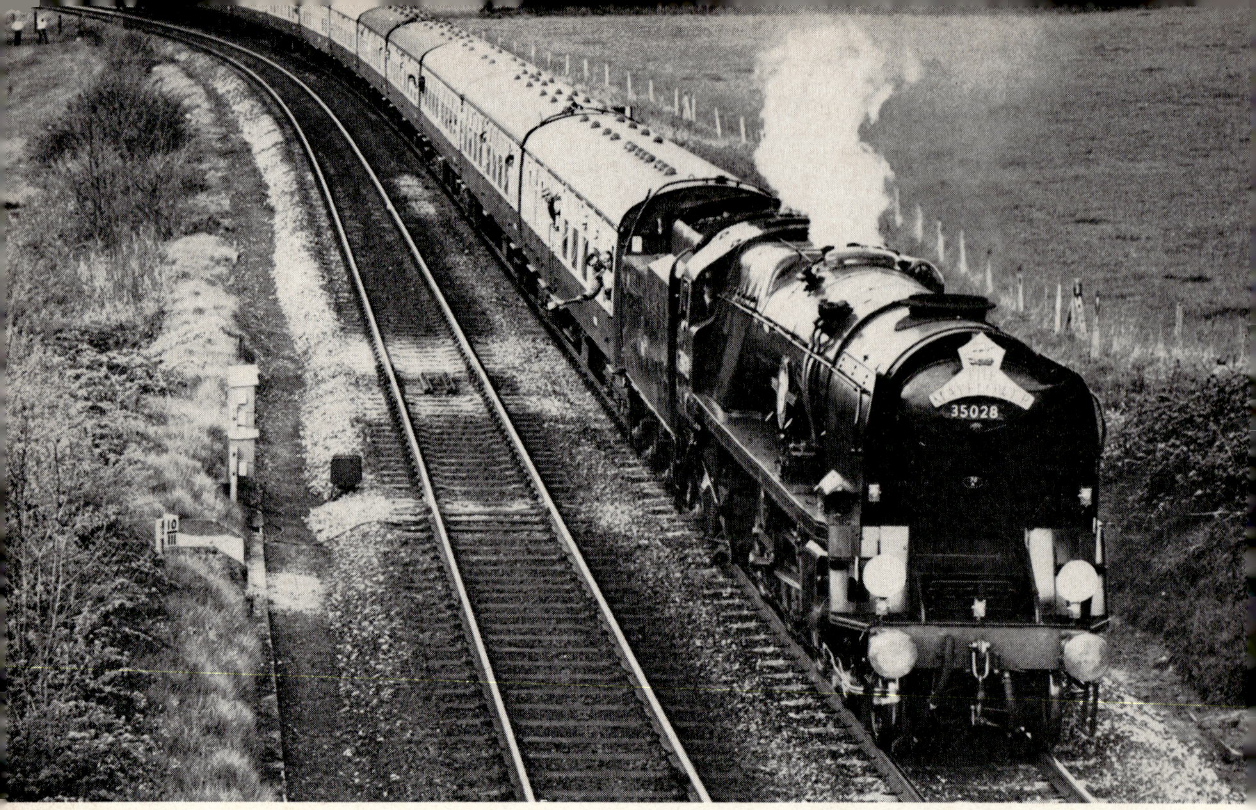
35028

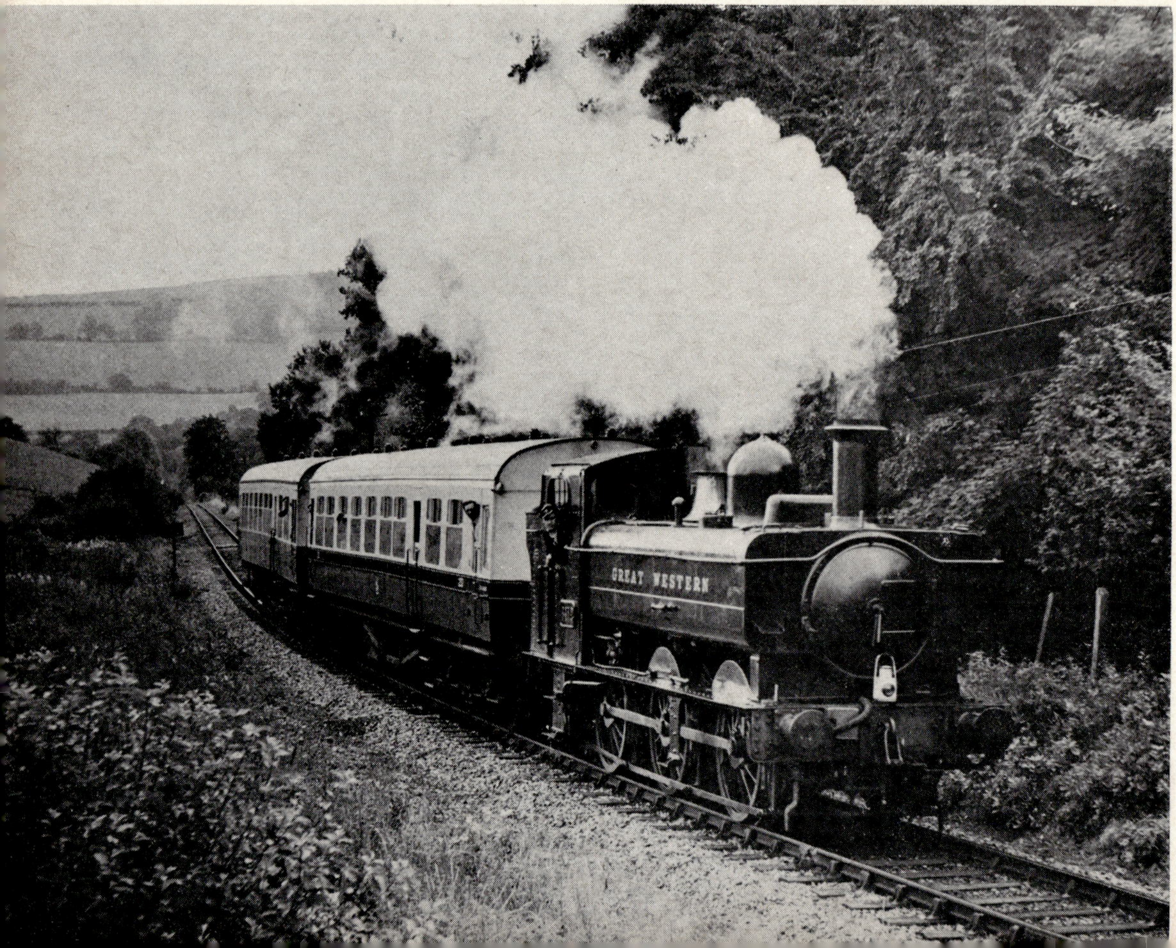
GREAT WESTERN

Left above: The Merchant Navy Preservation Society's ex-SR Pacific No 35028 *Clan Line* on a railtour special near Church Stretton in April 1975.
R. E. B. Siviter

Left: Dart Valley Railway's ex-GWR 0-6-0PT No 6412 approaching Buckfastleigh on a regular working in July 1970. *T. G. Flinders*

Above: Great Western Society's 4-6-0s Nos 7808 *Cookham Manor* and 6998 *Burton Agnes Hall* at Wyre Piddle on a society Didcot-Hereford excursion in June 1975. *L. A. Nixon*

Right: Dart Valley Railway's ex-GWR 2-6-2T No 4588 climbing to Greenway with a regular Kingswear-Paignton service in June 1974. *T. G. Flinders*

Left: Class 52 2700hp C-C diesel-hydraulic No 1040 *Western Queen* heading a Paddington-Penzance express up the last stage of Dainton Bank in July 1974.
G. F. Gillham

Above: No 1063 *Western Monitor* crossing from Cornwall into Devonshire over Brunel's Royal Albert Bridge with a Penzance-Paddington train in June 1974.
P. D. Hawkins

Left: Class 42 2200hp B-B diesel-hydraulic Warship No 825 *Intrepid* at Exeter St Davids with a Waterloo-Exeter train in June 1971.
N. E. Preedy

Right: Hymek 1700hp B-B diesel-hydraulic on an evening Paddington-Westbury train in October 1972 at Thatcham. *D. E. Canning*

Below: Hymek No 7037 on a Portsmouth-Bristol train at Westbury in August 1970. *Derek Cross*

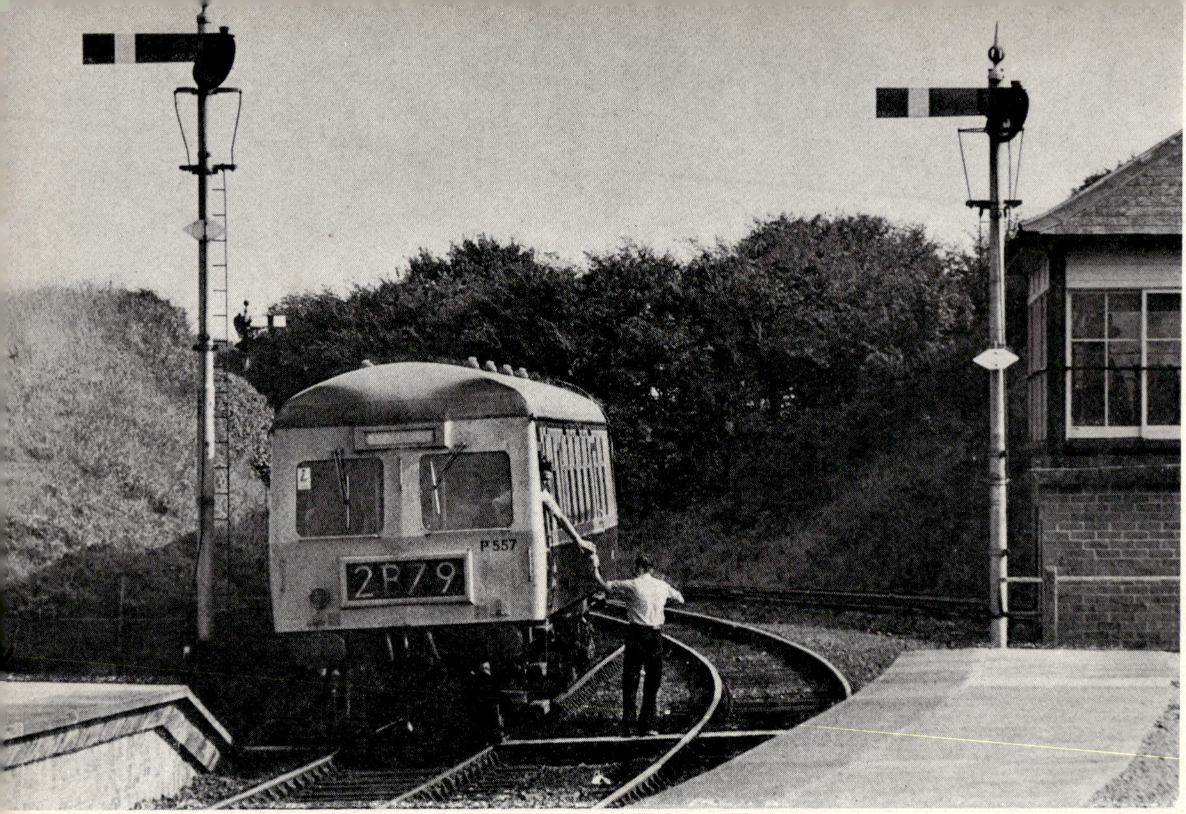
P557
2P79

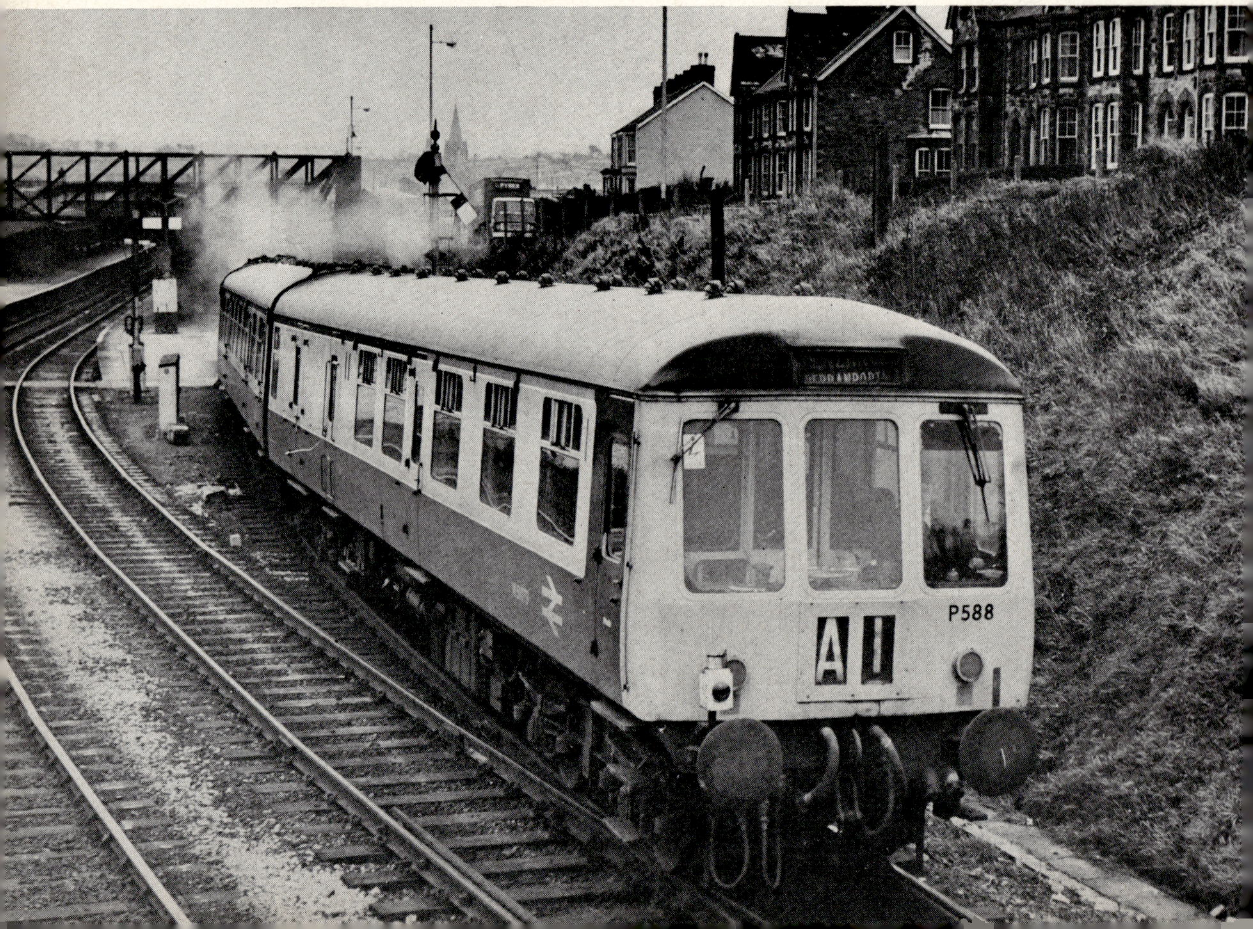
P588
A1

Left: Handing over the token as a Swindon three-car dmu forming a Par-Newquay train in September 1973 enters Newquay Station. *P. D. Hawkins*

Left below: Gloucester RCW three-car dmu on a Truro-Falmouth service leaving Truro Station in November 1974. *Brian Morrison*

Right: A Swindon cross-country dmu set minus trailer forming a Liskeard-Looe train approaching Coombe Junction in July 1975. *Graham B. Wise*

Below: One of the Metro-Cammell diesel-electric eight-car Pullman sets forming the South Wales Pullman passing Swindon in April 1972.
J. H. Cooper-Smith

Left: Class 47/4 No 47.492 (1760) takes a train of 100-ton tankers past the down sidings at Ebbw Junction, Newport, in April 1975. *P. D. Hawkins*

Far left below: No 47.229 (1905) wheels a westbound South Wales Freightliner on to the temporarily speed-restricted (20mph) Stapleton Road Bridge, Bristol, in May 1975. *P. J. Fowler*

Below: Class 37 Co-Cos Nos 37.301 (6601) and 37.304 (6604) approaching Newport (Gwent) Station with a Port Talbot-Llanwern (British Steel Corporation) train of 20 100-ton iron ore wagons in April 1975. The train is intended eventually to be formed of 27 such wagons and three Class 37s. *P. D. Hawkins*

Left: Class 52 No 1054 *Western Governor* passing Newton Abbot with an Etruria-St Blazey train of china clay empties in August 1971.   *David Wharton*

Below: Warship No 831 *Monarch* passing Newton Abbot with a special freight in August 1971.   *David Wharton*

Right: NBL Class 29 1100hp B-B diesel-hydraulic No 6330 climbing away from Tiverton Junction with an Exeter-Hemyock milk train in July 1970.   *John M. Boyes*

Right below: EE Class 20 1000hp Bo-Bo diesel-electric No 8073 (20.073) moves to the top of Lickey Incline in February 1970 after the brakes of its southbound freight have been pinned down.   *Anthony A. Vickers*

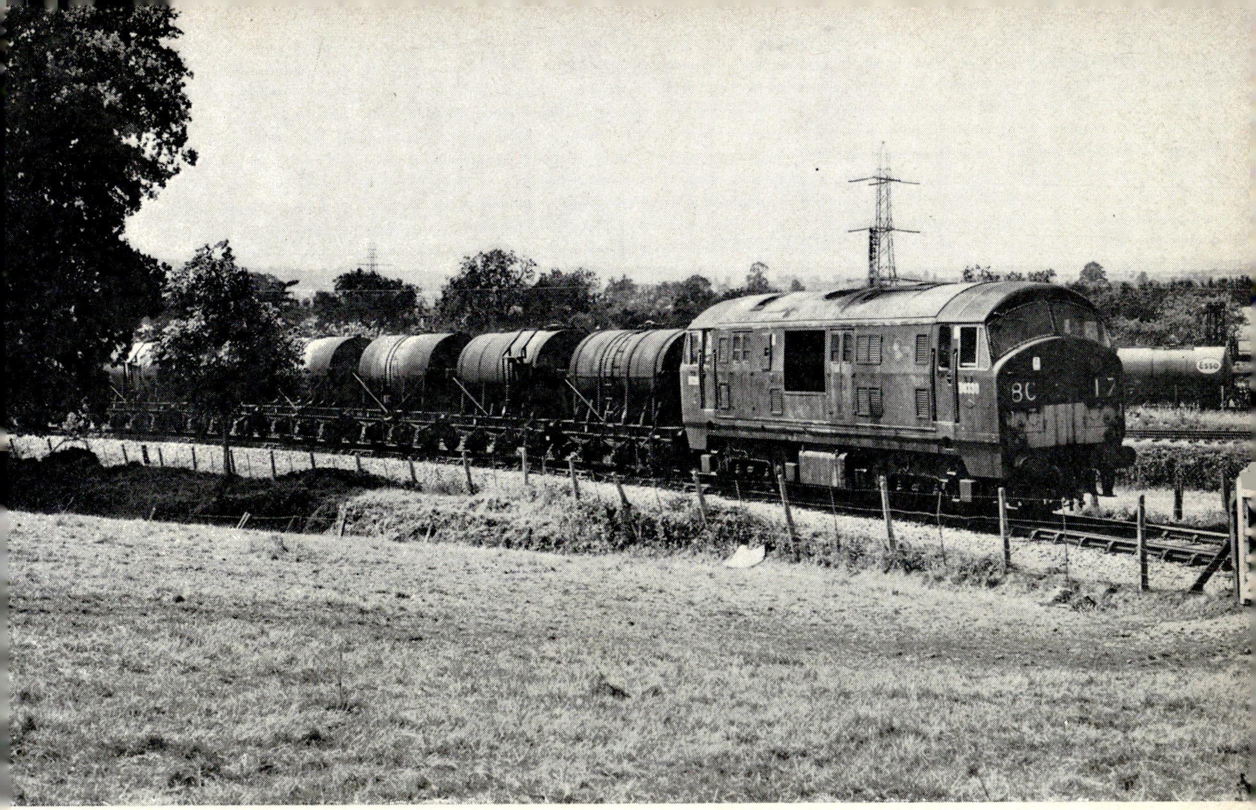
80
17
Esso

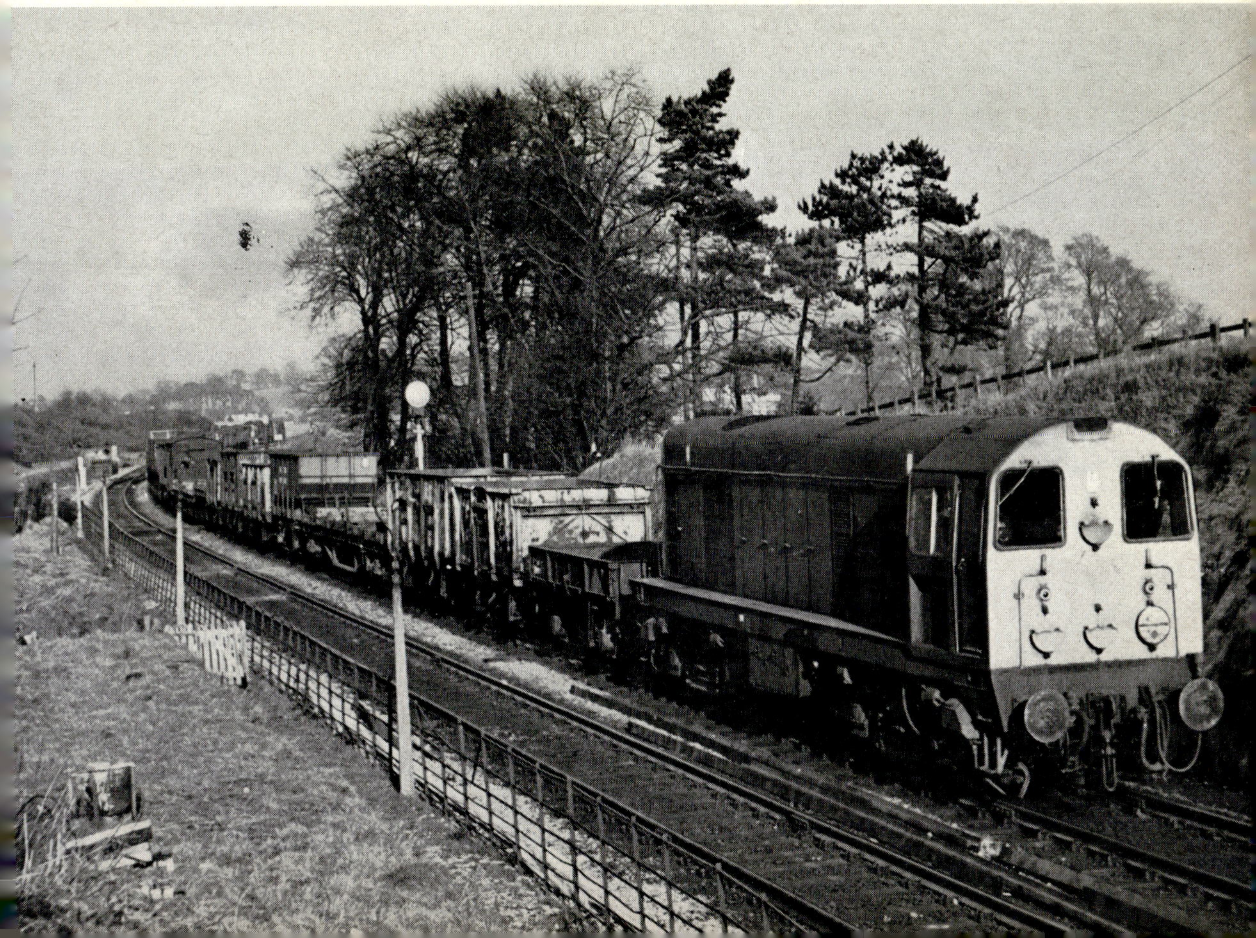

Above: Park Royal two-car dmu heading a southbound train passing Harlech Castle on the Cambrian Coast line in October 1971. *Vernon D. Shaw*

Left: Derby two-car dmu forming a Llandudno-Blaenau Festiniog train heading away from Pont-y-Pant along the Lledra Valley in April 1974.
A. W. Hobson

Right: Nicely timed picture at Minffordd of Class 24/15 Nos 5054 (24.054) and 5076 (24.076) hauling an 11-coach Wirral Railway Circle Crewe-Pwllheli special Cambrian Coast Express in December 1973, catching Festiniog Railway's Hunslet 0-4-0STs *Linda* and *Blanche* heading a Santa Special over the bridge. *G. R. Hounsell*

Above: EE Class 37 No 37.034 (6734) heading a Silcock & Colling Ford train down the grade from Patchway towards the Severn Tunnel in September 1974. *P. J. Fowler*

Right above: Class 46 Peak No 143 (46.006) taking the Gloucester avoiding line with a Paignton-Leeds train in July 1972. *N. E. Preedy*

Right: The unique Brush Falcon 2700hp Co-Co diesel-electric No 1200 at Royal Oak on a Paddington-Bristol train in July 1971.
J. H. Cooper-Smith

Last page: EE Class 50 No 50.003 (403) accelerates a Paddington-Weston-super-Mare train away from Bristol Temple Meads in September 1974.
P. J. Fowler

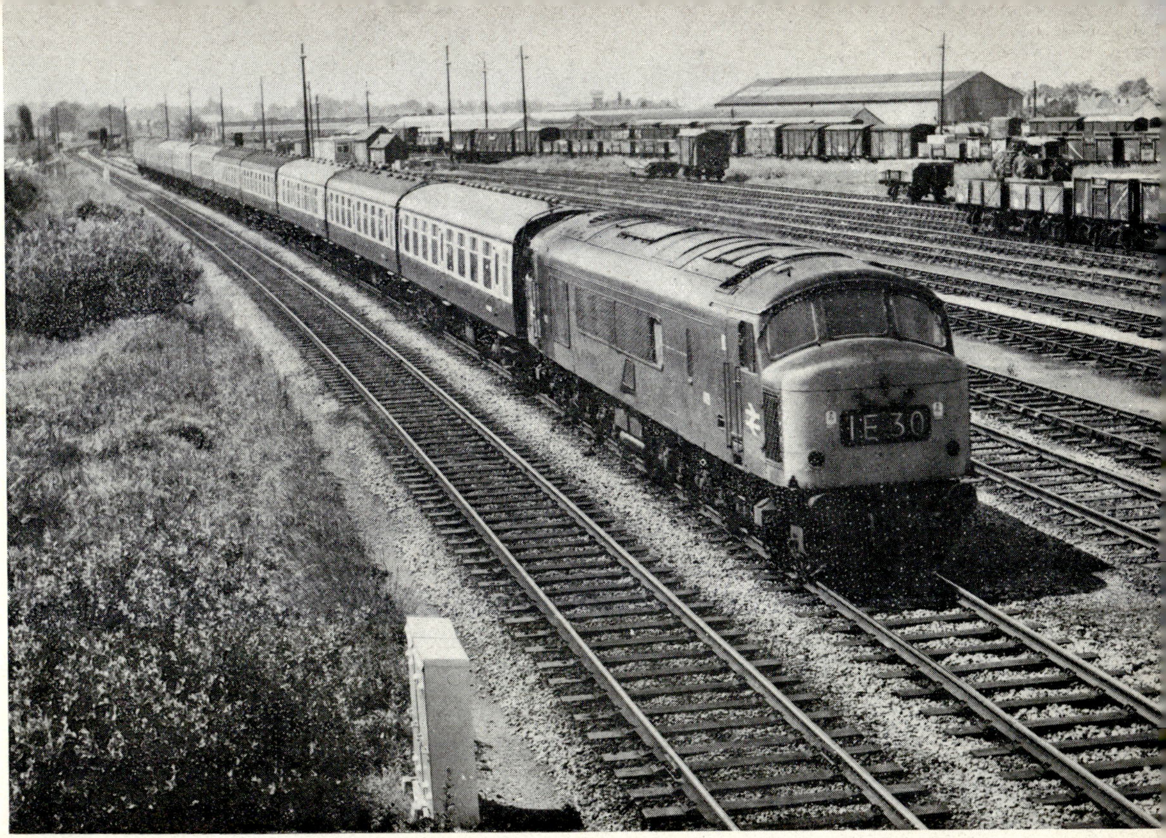
1E30

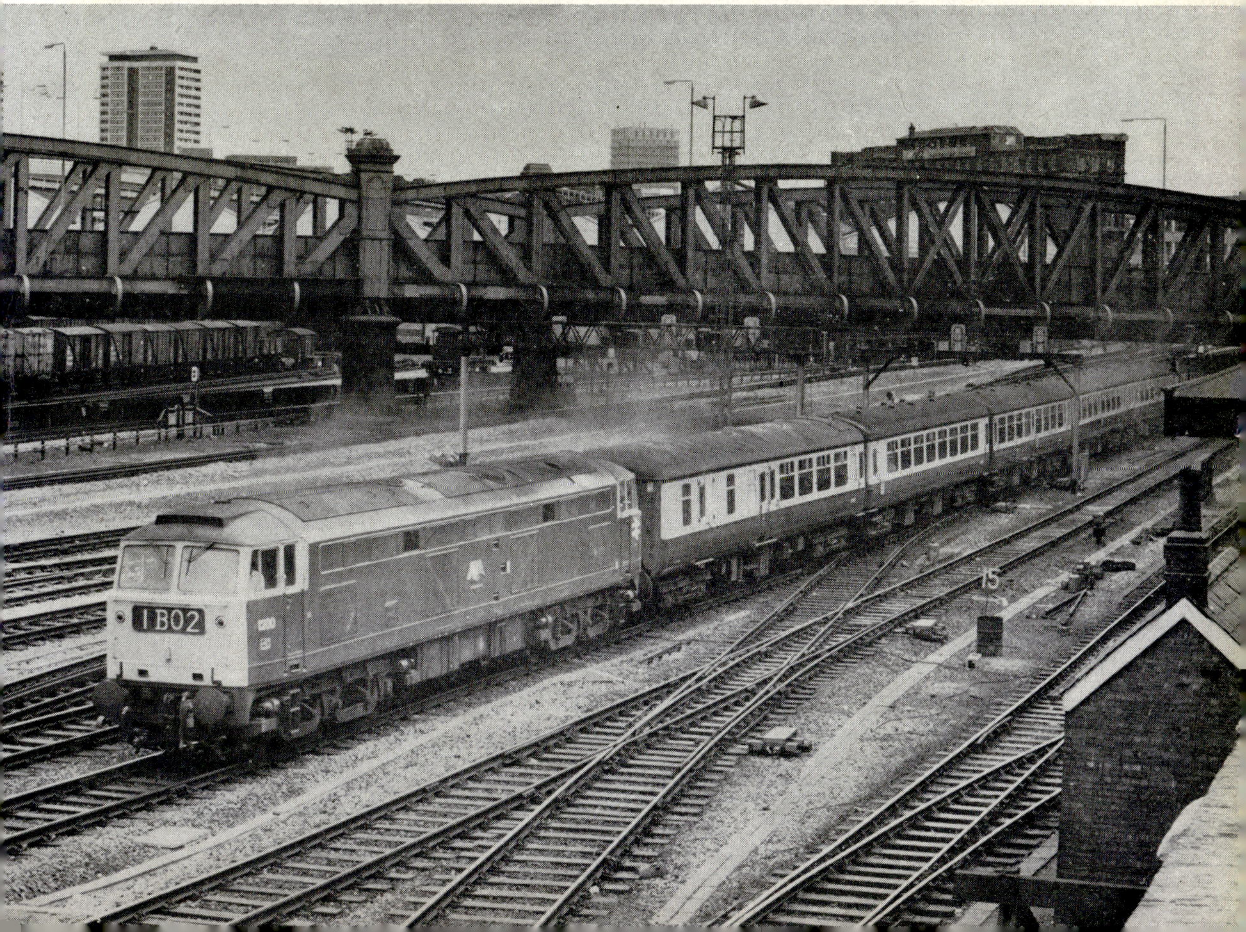
1B02
15